MW00353653

And now I know this mystery, that wrong-doers will twist and pervert the words of right doing in many ways, and will speak wicked words, and lie and practice great deceits, and write books concerning *their* words.

But when those write down truthfully all *my* words in their languages, and do not change or take away anything from my words but write them all down truthfully, all that I first testified concerning them, then I know another mystery that books will be given to the right-doers and the wise to become a cause of joy and uprightness and much wisdom. To them will the books be given. And they will believe in them and rejoice over them. Then will all the right-doers, who have learned from them all the paths of uprightness, be rewarded.

From Enoch 104

# Also by
# Timothy J. Sakach, Ph. D.

Enoch: The Book Behind the Bible

The Enoch Calendar with
Sabbaths, Feasts and High Days

Prophecy Unsealed!
The Great Destiny of Human Kind
as Prophesied by the Scriptures or
How to Prepare for the Coming New Age

# FATHERS

## THE TESTAMENTS OF THE
## TWELVE PATRIARCHS

A Revised and Edited Version
Based on the Translation of R. H. Charles

# Timothy J. Sakach, Ph. D.

**Innertech Publishing**
**Laguna Niguel, California**

Copyright © 2010 by Timothy J. Sakach, Ph.D.

All rights reserved.

Published by Innertech Publishing

PO Box 7560, Laguna Niguel, California 92607

First Edition

Web Site: Innertech.com

"Prepare the way ... " Blog Site: Innertech.com

No part of this publication may be reproduced, stored in a retrieval system or transmitted, in any form or by any means, electronic, mechanical, photocopying, recording, or otherwise, without the prior written permission of Innertech Publishing. The author reserves the right to substitute names from the original language and to emphasize words and phrases in Scriptural passages.

Keywords: History, Prophecy, Revelation, Spiritual, Scriptures, Prophets, End Age, Resurrection, Enoch, Daniel, Weeks, Righteous, Elect, Messengers. End Time

ISBN: 0-934917-09-4

EAN: 978-0-934917-09-4

Ver: 1.0

Manufactured in the United States of America

# Contents

# Preface

⧗

As I found with "Enoch: The Book Behind the Bible" the result was a refreshing new look at an old translation that the original translators may not have understood. That should not be a surprise or even taken to sound like disrespect to those who labored on that task. Nevertheless, a comment from one of the readers was, "I had a copy of this book in its original form, but I could not make heads or tails out of it. But your work conveys the sense that Enoch was trying to convey. Why is that?"

There are several problems that must be corrected. First, time and language evolved. Words that made sense 100 years ago are now obsolete. For example, how often today to you hear people say, "Hearken"? Some may go through life and never hear that word. Compare that with "Listen up!" or "Pay attention!" or "Hey, I am talking here!" These examples convey the meaning of "Hearken" in today's vernacular, do they not?

Second, what is so religious about King James English? This is particularly annoying in writing when someone speaks in dialogue, the narrator suddenly switches to "speaking to thee in words thou hath never used!" It becomes even more annoying when a Messenger from Heaven, who has been speaking for a long time before King James, suddenly jumps into 16th century English.

A third problem is the ancient use of very long run on sentences that contain punctuation like: this or that; followed by another; and that should have; been a but; only to carry over to, another thought, separated by a comma; leaving, of course, the reader nearly in – a coma; but I digress!

A fourth problem is a carry over from the original language, and that is the repeated use of "and," and that means that we may be reading a translation from Hebrew, and that may be of interest to scholars, and that is not a characteristic of the language you and I speak, and is that not correct?

Then we run into confusing chapter and verse structure. Do we need that to understand what the author is saying? If I were to tell you that thus and so was found in Reuben's testimony, shouldn't you be able to find it in the context?

The point is that these things regardless of the time in which they were written would benefit us the most if they were read as though they were written today, without changing the sense. And that is my objective.

In the not too distant past the Protestant clergy, particularly from England, preached and prayed in King James English. In fact, my mother, bless her, prayed all her life to her dying day in King James English.

But that was then, and yet there are still cultures that speak that way. But it really is out of context when it comes to spiritual matters, isn't it? Frankly, to most people, religious "talk" is "affected talk."

This also applies to the choice of vocabulary. For example, if I used the word "redemption." That is a noun, which in today's language might be, "the act of purchasing!" To say that one is "sanctified" doesn't mean the same as it did 100 years ago. Today, it might have no clear meaning. Technically it means "cleansed and set apart from the rest."

Finally, there is one other problem when working with ancient, translated documents — spotting the work of deceitful scribes carrying agendas. Such was the case here. Christian scribes, who were really untrained parishioners, felt they were "doing God a service" by adding phrases that described the "work of their Jesus!" Now you and I know that the name "Jesus" is Greek and comes from the Latin. Men speaking Hebrew, long before these "scribes" added their stuff, would not have said these things. Did these deceiver scribes really think that would fly? Because these made no sense and did not fit the context, I removed them. I thought at first that I should make footnotes out of them. But as I read them, I could not answer the question: Why? Then after they were removed, like a mystery had been solved, the real context spoke its message with clarity!

I want to thank my wife, Marina, who helps me find the space and time to tackle these projects. She has been a great blessing since the time I looked at her across the crowded room and saw the word "WIFE!" light up mysteriously in my mind's eye.

I also want to thank my brothers, Dan, Tom and Jon who also encouraged me by reading my books and providing me with much needed spontaneous feedback. And thanks to my son Stephen for his support in reaching many people through handling the advertising that helped bring my blog to one of the top 10 in its genre.

And a special thanks to the readers, (of my blog posts, letters, comments, and other books,) for their support and encouragement to write more and often.

# Introduction

T his book contains the "copies" of the testaments or last message (testimonies) of the fathers of the tribes of Israel. "Israel" was the name given to Jacob, son of Isaac. A 'Man' from Elohim came to Jacob when he was alone, and Jacob fought with him and refused to let him go until he agreed to bless Jacob. The Man caused Jacob's thigh to go out of joint, and then pronounced a blessing on him and said that his name would be "Israel"

> Your name is no longer called "Jacob," but "Israel"
> because you have striven with Elohim and with Men and
> have overcome."

The name "Israel" has more than one meaning and all of them apply:

> "To strive with EL,"
> "To overcome with EL,"
> "To rule with EL."

The name Israel is the blessing and from that time on, the descendants of Israel became a people who were set apart from the rest of the world. This concept of a "special people" is misunderstood by the rest of humanity.

The offspring of Jacob are the called "the Plant of Righteousness." That may seem strange because their actions through the ages may not have appeared as being righteous. For most of their history they were not. Ezekiel was told that they are a stubborn and hard-hearted people.

Even the life of the fathers as you will read was filled with problems, mistakes, and troubles. But yet the fathers realized that they were wrong, and they repented of their wickedness -- at least on their deathbeds.

Why then is Israel, the offspring of the sons of Jacob, set apart from the world? Certainly not because they grew into more profound righteousness. That did not happen. They grew more and more unrighteous.

To Moses and Yahua, the people were obnoxious and frustrating whiners. They were forever complaining and grumbling about all things. They even fashioned gods out of gold and worshipped them. They plotted against their leaders and each other. They committed incest, fornication, and adultery. And they plotted to kill one of their own, Joseph, because they were jealous and envious of him.

They were proud and refused to learn. And they became the most fierce people on earth. Their offspring still are.

What made the difference between their offspring and the rest of the world?

Their fathers.

In spite of some unfortunate errors by clumsy scribes, nearly all of the original information has remained. The errors and additions caused by the scribes was obvious. They tried to interject church related comments that only took away from the messages the fathers had for their offspring. The obvious Christian bias and phrases stood out like beacons. The "additions" were completely out of context to what the fathers were telling, and were obviously written sometime between 100 and 300 CE.

The relationship of the fathers to EL and Yahua becomes very clear when those Names replace the words "God" and "Lord," which do not carry the same precise meaning as the Hebrew.

EL is the One. The supreme and prime Father. From within His Being was born the SON. The Son then took from the essence and power of EL and made all things in the heavens and on the earth. This process formed a deep relationship with the line of fathers that started with Adam and continued through these men. As noted, the line was called the Plant of Righteousness.

We are, everyone, descendants of that line – at least starting with the Sons of Noah. Noah's great grandfather was Enoch.

Enoch's focus was on his descendants. So also is the focus of each of the fathers. You will find two bodies of listeners: the brothers, and the offspring or children. In each case a meeting is called between the father and the children to whom he gave his testimony. In most cases, it was also a time of confession and contrition and an exhortation by each father to his children to follow EL and Yahua and to not depart from the instructions of Yahua.

These men were not Jews. There was no "Jewish religion" at that time, contrary to popular opinion. Enoch was not a Jew, nor was Noah. None of Noah's sons were Jews. Abraham was not, and neither was either Isaac or Jacob. Jacob was given the name Israel, which does not make him a Jew. None of Jacob's sons were Jews, nor did any of these follow the Jewish religion. Also Moses was not a Jew nor was Joshua, or Aaron, the brother of Moses. This may sound like blasphemy to many people. But even Judah was not called a Jew.

However, after the Kingdom of Israel split, due to the oppressive rule of Rehoboam, Solomon's son. The people separated into the House of Israel and the House of Judah. After that the people of Judea or the House of Judah were looked upon as people from Judea or "Jews." The House of Judah consisted of the descendants of Judah, Benjamin, and part of the priestly tribe of Levi.

Before that time, there were no Jews or Jewish religion or Judaism!

But all of these men from Adam to the fathers had a deep spiritual relation with EL and EL's Son Yahua. As you will see, even though some serious mistakes were made, the most valued asset in each of their individual lives was their spiritual connection with the Elohim. It was this relationship that they desired to pass on to their children down through the ages -- even to our day!

Each testament follows the same pattern.

The statement of the "copy" as opposed to the "original."

The gathering of the sons.

Sometimes the calling of the brothers, if they were alive.

The confession of guilt and mistakes.

The exhortation to always follow EL and Yahua and their commandments and instructions.

Warning against falling away in the "end of days."

Instructions from each father, to bury his body with Abraham, and Isaac in the land that was promised.

All of these Testaments were given while they lived in Egypt. This introduces a spiritual significance that they wanted their children to learn. Egypt, which was a land of exile and oppression, was not and never would be home, whether in life or death. A land was promised to them by Yahua who promised it to them throughout their generations. Therefore, leaving the bodies of the fathers in Egypt was the ultimate sign of disrespect. Abraham hallowed the land by creating altars to Yahua in every place where he lived. The fathers new the significance of Abraham's and Isaac's faith and deep respect for Yahua. This land had been hallowed (set apart) by the drawing of lots and the lot fell to Shem (part of the Plant of Righteousness.)

So staying buried in Egypt was not an option. Nor was the land to be considered as "Canaan's land." Without question, it was Shem's land and belonged to Shem's offspring. The brothers of Shem (Ham and Japheth) were given other lands by lot. Canaan was the son of Ham. This division of the earth was also sealed by both an oath and a curse. The oath was that each would respect the lands as they were given. The curse was that if any one of their children who tried to take land belonging not to them but to another would be cursed and would not be able to make the land produce. Canaan took Shem's land, much to the dismay of his father Ham and his brothers. But later the offspring of Ham's other sons also moved in with Canaan.

There are songs about Canaan's land as though it was special to him and blessed. However, such was not the case. They experienced drought and famine. Bees, locusts, and lions would attack them. They found no peace or blessing while living there. And so it was and so it is to this day.

Not only is it NOT Canaan's land, but also it never was the land of the Philistines although it also carried the name "Palestine" (a version of the name Philistine). This has brought curses and lack of peace on these people. This entire process of the division of the earth is recorded in the Book of Jubilees.

During the time when Jacob's sons were born and matured in the land, the Canaanite wars broke out. It was primarily targeted against the family. All twelve of the fathers were born in the Land. The Canaanite tribes, though suffering while in the Land, decided to wage war against Jacob and his sons. But Jacob and his young sons (late teens and early twenties) withstood the Canaanites and continually defeated them in every battle.

But later famine came upon all the land and the surrounding peoples, and they fled to Egypt for help.

You will find many stories about how the brothers out of envy and jealousy plotted against Joseph and sold him to Ishmaelites who carried him off to Egypt. Then the brothers lied to Jacob and made him think that Joseph had been killed by an animal. Each of the fathers had a part in this crime. And some protected Joseph from the other brothers who wanted him dead.

Joseph's story was about his problems with Potiphar's wife who relentlessly tried to seduce him. His continual resistance nearly cost him his life, and he was imprisoned. It was this trial that showed the character and strength of Joseph, and why he was singled out and given a special blessing from Yahua.

Judah also had a different set of problems, which started when he took a Canaanite woman to be his wife! Then he sought a wife for his oldest son, Onan. The woman was Tamar, a relative of Abraham. But Judah's wife did not want her sons to have children from a Shemite and Hebrew. So she instructed them to not get her pregnant. Onan after sleeping with Tamar for a year complied by "pulling out," and he died. Then his brother married her, and did that same in compliance with his mother's wishes. He also died. Then the third son, said, "No, I am not stupid. I do not want anything to do with her."

In the end, Judah, was the one who got Tamar pregnant, and she gave birth to twins, from which came the race of Judah. He never had sex with her again.

Judah's history stands out from his brothers and because of his strength and zeal, he received the promise of kings. But Joseph received the promise of the birthright and prosperity.

It was these two "races" of Israel that carried the leadership and blessings forward to the other offspring of the sons of Jacob.

This history is like a bit of the wild west of American history. This was the original "Bonanza" family. The testaments are full of answers to questions for which the Scriptures only offer hints. What these men did forms the basis for the history of the Middle East. They laid down patterns that illustrated the problems that their genetics was going to bring upon their progeny. They warned of trouble that would come to them in the end of the days— our time. These prophecies and warnings are the focal point of the end time— prophesied to be the "time of Jacob's trouble, but he will be delivered out of it."

The secret to the promised deliverance was different in detail and focus but always the same from each of the fathers: follow the instructions (Torah) of Yahua, and pray to EL. Those instructions are the same as recorded by the Prophets and Apostles many centuries later. It is the same now. Nothing has changed. The relationship with EL and Yahua is what saved them. That same faithfulness, commitment, and trust applies not only to their descendants, but also to the rest of mankind regardless of what they believe now.

These men repented of the bad things they thought and did. Those of them who held fast and did not sin, were blessed and delivered, and this blessing carries over to their offspring in this day.

Abraham was promised that his offspring would be as the sand of the sea in number. The children of Israel who were delivered by Yahua from the oppression of Egypt became as the sand of sea and as numerous as the stars, but they refused to heed the warnings of their fathers. As a result they were scattered among the gentile nations. They learned from the nations, rather than from their fathers. They became unclean. They lost the knowledge that they really are the "Plant of Righteousness" in this world wherever they live.

But they have not been forgotten. Yahua ("He exists!") also called "The Son of MAN" came to the earth to fulfill the requirements of the covenant He made with them when He brought them out of Egypt. At that time He said that He placed before them blessings and curses, life and death. And He encouraged them to chose "Life, that both you and your seed may live." Their actions betrayed them and caused them to choose death.

Now we are faced with one of the greatest deliverance stories that human kind will ever know and realize. Yahua purchased not only the people of the covenant— the Plant of Righteousness, but because they stood as proxy for the all humanity, He bought all by paying the price that was on their head. Therefore, everyone became His possession. As He said, "I own the gold and the silver." And of course, He owns everything and everyone.

But first, it will start with the Sons of promise— the fathers, and the fathers' fathers. It was the Sons who agreed to become Kings and Priests in the world. They replied, "All that Yahua says we will do!" Yahua did not reply. He knew, and I imagine He might have thought something like, "You certainly will."

Where are these people today?

In American, Canada, England, Ireland, Scotland, Israel, Norway, Sweden, Denmark, France, Spain, Switzerland, the Baltic States, Germany, Poland, Russia, Eastern Europe, Australia, New Zealand, South Africa, and on and on in hundreds of nations around the world. They have been dispersed among the gentiles. Some received the label "Caucasian," referring to the path many trod. Others moved out of the promised land by ship and caravan to settle in remote parts of the earth, unknown to their mind who their fathers are and the great spiritual heritage of which all of them are heirs. And with them came their helpers who helped them carry their burdens and their children, just as happened to the original family when they were brought out of Egypt.

*"Children, listen carefully with full attention*
*to the words of your fathers ..."*

FATHERS: THE TESTAMENTS OF THE TWELVE PATRIARCHS

# The Testament of Reuben

## The Firstborn Son of Jacob and Leah

The copy of the Testament of Reuben, even the commands which he gave his sons before he died in the hundred and twenty-fifth year of his life. Two years after the death of Joseph his brother, when Reuben fell ill, his sons and his sons' sons were gathered together to visit him. And he said to them:

My children, See! I am dying, and go the way of my fathers. And seeing there Judah, and Gad, and Asher, his brothers, he said to them: Raise me up, that I may tell to my brothers and to my children what things I have hidden in my heart, for see, now at length I am passing away.

And he arose and kissed them, and said to them: Hear, my brothers, and you, my children, give ear to Reuben your father in the commands which I give to you. And look, I call to witness against you this day, the EL of heaven, that you walk not in the sins of youth and fornication, wherein I was poured out, and defiled the bed of my father Jacob. And I tell you that he smote me with a sore plague in my loins for seven months; and had not my father Jacob prayed for me to Yahua, Yahua would have destroyed me. For I was thirty years old when I wrought the evil thing before Yahua, and for seven months I was sick to death.

And after this I repented with set purpose of my soul for seven years before Yahua. And I did not drink wine and strong drink, and flesh did not enter into my mouth, and I ate no pleasant food; but I mourned over my sin, for it was great, such as had not been in Israel.

And now hear me, my children, what things I saw concerning the seven spirits of deceit, when I repented. Seven spirits therefore are appointed against man, and they are the leaders in the works of youth.

First, the spirit of fornication is seated in the nature and in the senses;

Second, the spirit of insatiableness in the belly;

Third, the spirit of fighting in the liver and gall.

Fourth is the spirit of obsequiousness and chicanery, that through officious attention one may be fair in seeming.

Fifth is the spirit of pride, that one may be boastful and arrogant.

Sixth is the spirit of lying, in perdition and jealousy to practise deceits, and concealments from kindred and friends.

Seventh is the spirit of injustice, with which are thefts and acts of rapacity, that a man may fulfill the desire of his heart; for injustice works together with the other spirits by the taking of gifts.

And with all these the spirit of sleep is joined which is (that) of error and fantasy.]

And so perishes every young man, darkening his mind from the truth, and not understanding the law of EL, nor obeying the admonitions of his fathers as befell me also in my youth.

And now, my children, love the truth, and it will preserve you: hear you the words of Reuben your father. Pay no heed to the face of a woman, Nor associate with another man's wife, Nor meddle with affairs of womankind.

For had I not seen Bilhah bathing in a covered place, I had not fallen into this great iniquity. For my mind taking in the thought of the woman's nakedness, caused me to not sleep until I had wrought the abominable thing.

For while Jacob our father had gone to Isaac his father, when we were in Eder, near to Ephrath in Bethlehem, Bilhah became drunk and was asleep uncovered in her chamber. Having therefore gone in and beheld nakedness, I wrought the impiety without her perceiving it, and leaving her sleeping I departed.

And immediately a Messenger of EL revealed to my father concerning my impiety, and he came and mourned over me, and touched her no more.

Pay no heed, therefore, my children, to the beauty of women, nor set your mind on their affairs; but walk in singleness of heart in the fear of Yahua, and expend labor on good works, and on study, and on your flocks, until Yahua give you a wife, whom He will, that you do not suffer as I did.

For until my father's death I could not look in his face or  speak to any of my brothers, because of the reproach. Even until now my conscience causes me anguish on account of my impiety.

And yet my father comforted me much and prayed for me to Yahua, that the anger of Yahua might pass from me, even as Yahua showed. And from that time until now I have been on my guard and did not sin.

Therefore, my children, I say to you, observe all things whatever I command you, and you shall not sin. For a pit to the soul is the sin of fornication, separating us from EL, and bringing us near to idols, because it deceives the mind and understanding,  and leads young men into the grave before their time. For fornication has destroyed many, because, though a man be old or noble, or rich or poor, he brings reproach upon himself with the sons of men and derision with Beliar.

For you heard regarding Joseph how he guarded himself from a woman, and purged his thoughts from all fornication, and found favor in the sight of EL and men.

For the Egyptian woman did many things to him, and summoned magicians, and offered him love potions, but the purpose of his soul admitted no evil desire. Therefore the EL of your fathers delivered him from every evil (and) hidden death. For if fornication does not overcome your mind, neither can Beliar overcome you.

For there are evil women, my children; and since they have no power or strength over man, they use wiles by outward attractions that they may draw him to themselves. And whom they cannot bewitch by outward attractions, him they overcome by craft.

For moreover, concerning them, the Messenger of Yahua told me, and taught me, that women are overcome by the spirit of fornication more than men, and in their heart they plot against men; and by means of their adornment they deceive first their minds, and by the glance of the eye instill the poison, and then through the accomplished act they take them captive.

For a woman cannot force a man openly, but by a harlot's bearing she beguiles him. Therefore flee fornication, my children, and command your wives and your daughters that they do not adorn their heads and faces to deceive the mind. Because every woman who uses these wiles has been reserved for eternal punishment.

For in this way they allured the Watchers who were before the flood. For as these continually looked at them, they lusted after them, and they conceived the act in their mind. For they changed themselves into the shape of men, and appeared to them when they were with their husbands. And the women lusting in their minds after their forms, gave birth to giants, for the Watchers appeared to them as reaching even to heaven.

Therefore beware of fornication; and if you wish to be pure in mind, guard your senses from every woman.

And command the women likewise to not associate with men, that they also may be pure in mind. For constant meetings, even though the ungodly deed is not done, are to them an irremediable disease, and to us a destruction of Beliar and an eternal reproach.

For in fornication there is neither understanding nor godliness, and all jealousy dwells in the lust that is part of it.

Therefore, I say to you, you will be jealous against the sons of Levi, and will seek to be exalted over them; but you shall not be able. For EL will avenge them, and you shall die by an evil death. For to Levi EL gave the sovereignty [of the priesthood].

Therefore I command you to pay attention to Levi, because he shall know the law of Yahua, and shall give ordinances for judgment and shall sacrifice for all Israel until the consummation of the times, as the anointed High Priest, of whom Yahua spake, "I adjure you by the EL of heaven to do truth each one to his neighbor and to entertain love each one for his brother."

And draw near to Levi in humbleness of heart, that you may receive a blessing from his mouth. For he shall bless Israel and Judah, because Yahua chose him to be king over all the nation. And bow down before his seed, for on our behalf it will die in wars visible and invisible, and will be among you an eternal king.

And Reuben died, having given these commands to his sons. And they placed him in a coffin until they carried him up from Egypt, and buried him in Hebron in the cave where his father was.

# The Testament of Simeon

## The Second Son of Jacob and Leah

⌛

The copy of the words of Simeon, the things that he spoke to his sons before he died, in the hundred and twenties year of his life, at which time Joseph, his brother, died. When Simeon was sick, his sons came to visit him, and he strengthened himself and sat up and kissed them, and said:

Pay attention, my children, to Simeon your father, And I will declare to you what things I have in my heart. I was born of Jacob as my father's second son; And my mother Leah called me Simeon, because Yahua had heard her prayer.

Furthermore, I became exceedingly strong. I shrank from no achievement, Nor was I afraid of anything. For my heart was hard, and my liver was immovable, and my bowels without compassion. Because valor also has been given from the Most High to men in soul and body.

In the time of my youth I was jealous in many things of Joseph, because my father loved him beyond all. And I set my mind against him to destroy him, because the prince of deceit sent forth the spirit of jealousy and blinded my mind, so that I did not regard Joseph as a brother, nor did I spare even Jacob my father.

But his EL and the EL of his fathers sent forth His Messenger, and delivered him out of my hands. For when I went to Shechem to bring ointment for the flocks, and Reuben to Dothan, where our necessaries and all our stores were, Judah my brother sold him to the

Ishmaelites.

And when Reuben heard these things he was grieved, for he wished to restore him to his father. But on hearing this I was exceedingly angered against Judah in that he let him go away alive, and for five months I continued to be angry against him.

But Yahua restrained me, and withheld from me the power of my hands; for my right hand was half withered for seven days. And I knew, my children, that because of Joseph this had happened to me, and I repented and wept; and I besought Yahua of Elohim that my hand might be restored, and that I might hold aloof from all pollution and envy and from all folly. For I knew that I had devised an evil thing before Yahua and Jacob my father, on account of Joseph my brother, whom I envied.

And now, my children, listen carefully to me and beware of the spirit of deceit and envy. For envy rules over the whole mind of a man, and does not allow him to eat or to drink, or to do any good thing. But it relentlessly suggests (to him) to destroy the one that he envies; and as long as he that is envied flourishes, he that envies fades away.

Two years therefore I afflicted my soul with fasting in the fear of Yahua, and I learned that deliverance from envy comes by the fear of EL. For if a man flees to Yahua, the evil spirit runs away from him, and his mind is lightened. And from that time on he sympathises with him whom he envied and forgives those who are hostile to him, and so he ceases from his envy.

And my father asked concerning me, because he saw that I was sad; and I said to him, I am pained in my liver. For I mourned more than they all, because I was guilty of the selling of Joseph. And when we went down into Egypt, and he bound me as a spy, I knew that I was suffering justly, and that I had not grieved.

Now Joseph was a good man, and had the Spirit of EL within him: being compassionate and pitiful, he bore no malice against me, but loved me even as the rest of his brothers. Therefore, beware, my children, of all jealousy and envy, and walk in singleness of soul and with good heart. Keep in mind Joseph, your father's brother, that EL may give you also grace and glory and blessing upon your heads even as you saw in Joseph's case. All his days he did not reproach us concerning this thing, but loved us as his own soul, and beyond his own sons glorified us, and gave us riches, and cattle and fruits.

Also, my children, love each one his brother with a good heart and the spirit of envy will withdraw from you. For envy makes savage the soul and destroys the body. It causes anger and war in the mind, and stirs it up to deeds of blood, and leads the mind into frenzy, and does not allow prudence to act in men. Moreover, it takes away sleep. For even in sleep some malicious jealousy, deluding him, gnaws and with wicked spirits disturbs his soul, and causes the body to be troubled, and wakes the mind from sleep in confusion. As a wicked and poisonous spirit, so it appears to men.

Therefore Joseph was handsome in appearance and pleasant to look upon, because no wickedness dwelt in him. for some of the trouble of the spirit the face displays.

And now, my children, make your hearts good before Yahua, and your ways straight before men. Then you shall find grace before Yahua and men.

Beware, therefore, of fornication because fornication is the mother of all evils, causing separation from EL and bringing near to Beliar. For I have seen it inscribed in the writing of Enoch that your sons shall be corrupted in fornication, and shall do harm to the sons of Levi with the sword. But they shall not be able to withstand Levi because he shall wage the war of Yahua, and shall conquer all your armies, and they shall become few in number, divided in Levi and Judah, and there shall be none of you for sovereignty, even as also our father prophesied in his blessings.

See, I have told you all things that I may be acquitted of your sin. Now, if you remove from you your envy and all stiff-neckedness, then as a rose shall my bones flourish in Israel, and as a lily my flesh in Jacob, And my odor shall be as the odor of Libanus. And as cedars shall holy ones be multiplied from me forever. Their branches shall stretch afar off. Then the seed of Canaan shall perish , and a remnant shall not be to Amalek. And all the Cappadocians shall perish, And all the Hittites shall be utterly destroyed.

Then shall fail the land of Ham, And all the people shall perish. Then shall all the earth rest from trouble, And all the world under heaven from war. Then the Mighty One of Israel shall glorify Shem, For Yahua of Elohim shall appear on earth and Himself save men.

Then shall all the spirits of deceit be given to be trodden under foot, and men shall rule over wicked spirits.

Then shall I arise in joy, and will bless the Most High because of his marvellous works. And now, my children, obey Levi and Judah, and do not be lifted up against these two tribes, for from them shall arise to you the salvation of EL. For Yahua shall raise up from Levi,  a High-priest, and from Judah,  a King. He shall save all the race of Israel. Therefore I give you these commands that you also may command your children that they may observe them throughout their generations.

And when Simeon had made an end of commanding his sons, he slept with his fathers, being an hundred and twenty years old. And they laid him in a wooden coffin, to take up his bones to Hebron. And they took them up secretly during a war of the Egyptians. For the bones of Joseph the Egyptians guarded in the tombs of the kings. For the sorcerers told them that on the departure of the bones of Joseph there should be throughout all the land darkness and gloom, and an exceeding great plague to the Egyptians, so that even with a lamp a man should not recognize his brother.

And the sons of Simeon bewailed their father. And they were in Egypt until the day of their departure by the hand of Moses.

FATHERS: THE TESTAMENTS OF THE TWELVE PATRIARCHS

# The Testament of Levi

## The Third Son of Jacob and Leah

T he copy of the words of Levi, the things which he ordained to his sons, according to all that they should do, and what things should befall them until the day of judgement. He was sound in health when he called them to him; for it had been revealed to him that he should die. And when they were gathered together he said to them:

I, Levi, was born in Haran, and I came with my father to Shechem. I was young, about twenty years of age, when, with Simeon, I wrought vengeance on Hamor for our sister Dinah.

When I was feeding the flocks in Abel-Maul, the spirit of understanding of Yahua came upon me, and I saw all men corrupting their way, and that unrighteousness had built for itself walls, and lawlessness sat upon towers. I was grieving for the race of the sons of men, and I prayed to Yahua that I might be saved. Then there fell upon me a sleep, and I saw a high mountain, and I was upon it.

Then I saw the heavens were opened and an Messenger of EL said to me, "Levi enter." And I entered from the first heaven, and I saw there a great sea hanging. And further I saw a second heaven far brighter and more brilliant, for a boundless light was also there.

And I said to the Messenger, "Why Is this so? "

And the Messenger said to me, "Do not marvel at this, for you shall see another heaven more brilliant and incomparable. And when you have ascended there, you shall stand near Yahua, and shall be His minister, and shall declare His mysteries to men, You shall proclaim concerning Him that which shall redeem Israel. By you and Judah shall Yahua appear among men saving every race of men. From Yahua's portion shall be your life, and He shall be your field and vineyard, and fruits, gold, and silver.

"Hear, therefore, regarding the heavens that have been shown to you. The lowest is gloomy to you because in that it shows all the unrighteous deeds of men. And it has fire, snow, and ice made ready for the day of judgement, in the righteous judgement of EL. In it are all the spirits of the "pay back" for vengeance on men.

"And in the second are the hosts of the armies which are ordained for the day of judgement, to work vengeance on the spirits of deceit and of Beliar. And above them are the holy ones.

"In the highest of all dwells the Great Glory, far above all holiness. In it are the archMessengers who minister and make atoning sacrifices to Yahua for all the sins of ignorance of the righteous – offering to Yahua a sweet-smelling savour, a reasonable and a bloodless offering.

"And [in the heaven below this] are the Messengers who carry answers to the Messengers of the presence of Yahua.

"In the heaven next to this are thrones and dominions in which they always offer praise to EL. Therefore when Yahua looks upon us, all of us are shaken. The heavens. the earth, and the abysses are shaken at the presence of His majesty. But the sons of men, having no perception of these things, sin and provoke the Most High.

"Now, therefore, know that Yahua shall execute judgment upon the sons of men. Because when the rocks are being broken and the sun becomes dark and the waters are dried up and the fire is going out and all creation troubled and the invisible spirits melting away and the grave takes spoils through the visitations of the Most High, men will be unbelieving and persist in their iniquity. Because of this with punishment shall they be judged.

"Therefore the Most High has heard your prayer, to separate you from iniquity and that you should become to Him a son and a servant and a minister of His presence.

"The light of knowledge shall you light up in Jacob, and as the sun shall you be to all the seed of Israel.

"And there shall be given to you a blessing, and to all your seed until Yahua shall visit all the Gentiles in His tender mercies for ever.

"Therefore there have been given to you counsel and understanding that you might instruct your sons concerning this. Because they that bless Him shall be blessed, and they that curse Him shall perish."

And upon this the Messenger opened to me the gates of heaven, and I saw the holy temple, and sitting on a throne of glory, the Most High.

And He said to me, "Levi, I have given you the blessings of the priesthood until I come and sojourn in the midst of Israel."

Then the Messenger brought me down to the earth, and gave me a shield and a sword, and said to me: "Execute vengeance on Shechem because of Dinah, your sister, and I will be with you because Yahua hath sent me."

And I destroyed at that time the sons of Hamor, as it is written in the heavenly tables.

And I said to him, "I pray you, O Lord, tell me your name, that I may call upon you in a day of tribulation."

And he said, "I am the Messenger who intercedes for the nation of Israel that they may not be smitten utterly for every evil spirit attacks it."

And after these things I awoke and blessed the Most High, and the Messenger who intercedes for the nation of Israel and for all the righteous.

When I was going to my father, I found a brazen shield where also the name of the mountain is Aspis, which is near Gebal to the south of Abila. And I kept these words in my heart.

After this I counselled my father, and Reuben my brother, to bid the sons of Hamor not to be circumcised for I was zealous because of the abomination which they had wrought on my sister. And I slew Shechem first, and Simeon slew Hamor. After this my brothers came and smote that city with the sword.

And my father heard these things and was angry and grieved in that they had received the circumcision and after that had been put to death. And in his blessings he looked amiss upon us for we sinned because we had done this thing against his will, and he was sick on that day.

But I saw that the sentence of EL was for evil upon Shechem for they sought to do to Sarah and Rebecca as they had done to Dinah our sister, but Yahua prevented them. And they persecuted Abraham our father when he was a stranger, and they vexed his flocks when they were big with young. And Eblaen, who was born in his house, they most shamefully handled. And they did this to all strangers, taking away their wives by force, and they banished them. But the wrath of Yahua came upon them to the uttermost.

And I said to my father Jacob, "By you will Yahua despoil the Canaanites, and will give their land to you and to your seed after you. For from this day forward shall Shechem be called a city of imbeciles. For as a man mocks a fool, so did we mock them. because also they had brought folly in Israel by defiling my sister."

And we departed and came to Bethel.

And there again I saw a vision as the former, after we had spent there seventy days. And I saw seven men in white raiment saying to me, "Arise, put on the robe of the priesthood, the crown of righteousness, the breastplate of understanding, the garment of truth, the plate of faith, the turban of the head, and the ephod of prophecy."

And they severally carried (these things) and put (them,) on me, and said to me. "From this time on become a priest of Yahua, you and your seed forever."

And the first anointed me with holy oil, and gave to me the staff of judgment.

The second washed me with pure water, and fed me with bread and wine (even) the most holy things, and clad me with a holy and glorious robe.

The third clothed me with a linen vestment like an ephod.

The fourth put round me a girdle like to purple.

The fifth gave me a branch of rich olive.

The sixth placed a crown on my head.

The seventh placed on my head a diadem of priesthood, and filled my hands with incense that I might serve as priest to Yahua of Elohim.

And they said to me, "Levi, your seed shall be divided into three offices for a sign of the glory of Yahua who is to come. And the first portion shall be great; yes, greater than it shall none be. The second shall be in the priesthood. And the third shall be called by a new name because a king shall arise in Judah, and shall establish a new priesthood, after the fashion of the Gentiles. and His presence is beloved as a prophet of the Most High of the seed of Abraham our father. Therefore, every desirable thing in Israel shall be for you and for your seed. You shall eat everything fair to look upon, and the table of Yahua shall your seed apportion. Some of them shall be high priests, judges, and scribes, for by their mouth shall the holy place be guarded."

And when I awoke, I understood that this (dream) was like the first dream. And I hid this also in my heart and told it not to any man upon the earth.

And after two days Judah and I went up with our father Jacob to Isaac our father's father. And my father's father blessed me according to all the words of the visions that I had seen. But he would not come with us to Bethel.

And when we came to Bethel, my father saw a vision concerning me that I should be their priest to EL. And he rose up early in the morning and paid tithes of all to Yahua through me.

And so we came to Hebron to dwell there. And Isaac called me continually to teach me the law of Yahua, just as the Messenger of Yahua showed to me.

And he taught me the law of the priesthood, of sacrifices, whole burnt-offerings, first-fruits, freewill-offerings, peace-offerings.

Each day he was instructing me and was busy on my behalf before Yahua, and said to me, "Beware of the spirit of fornication; for this shall continue and shall by your seed pollute the holy place. Take, therefore, to yourself a wife without blemish or pollution, while you are young, and not of the race of strange nations.

"And before entering into the holy place, bathe; and when you offer the sacrifices wash. And again, when you finished the sacrifice, wash. Of twelve trees having leaves, offer to Yahua, as Abraham taught me also. And of every clean beast and bird offer a sacrifice to Yahua. And of all your first-fruits and of wine, offer the first, as a sacrifice to Yahua of Elohim, and every sacrifice you shall salt with salt.

"Now, therefore, tell what I command you to your children for what things I have heard from my fathers I have told to you. And see, I am clear from your ungodliness and transgression, which you shall commit in the end of the ages. For you shall deceive Israel, and stir up against it great evils from Yahua. And you shall deal lawlessly together with Israel, so He shall not bear with Jerusalem because of your wickedness. And you shall be scattered as captives among the Gentiles, and shall be for a reproach and for a curse there."

Therefore I took a wife when I was twenty-eight years old, and her name was Melcha. And she conceived and bare a son, and I called his name Gersam, for we were sojourners in our land. And I saw concerning him, that he would not be in the first rank, And Kohath was born in the thirty-fifth year of my life, towards sunrise. And I saw in a vision that he was standing on high in the midst of all the congregation, Therefore I called his name Kohath [which is, "beginning of majesty and instruction"]. And she bare me a third son, in the fortieth year of my life; and since his mother bare him with difficulty, I called him Merari, that is, 'my bitterness,' because he also was near to death. And Jochebed was born in Egypt in my sixty-fourth year for I was renowned then in the midst of my brothers.

And Gersam took a wife, and she bare to him Lomni and Semei.

And the sons of Kohath, Ambram, Issachar, Hebron, and Ozeel.

And the sons of Merari, Mooli, and Mouses.

And in the ninety-fourth year Ambram took Jochebed my daughter to him to wife, for they were born in one day, he and my daughter.

Eight years old was I when I went into the land of Canaan, and eighteen years when I slew Shechem, and at nineteen years I became priest, and at twenty-eight years I took a wife, and at forty-eight I went into Egypt.

And see, my children, you are a third generation. In my hundred and eighteenth year Joseph died.

And now, my children, I command you: Fear Yahua your Elohim with your whole heart, And walk in simplicity according to all His law. And also teach your children

letters that they may have understanding all their life,
Reading unceasingly the law of EL. For every one that
knows the law of Yahua shall be honoured, And shall not
be a stranger whereever he goes. Yes, many friends shall
he gain, even more than his parents, And many men shall
desire to serve him, And to hear the law from his mouth.
Therefore sork righteousness, my children, upon the earth
that you may have (it) as a treasure in heaven.

And sow good things in your souls, That you may find
them in your life. But if you sow evil things, You shall reap
every trouble and affliction.

Get wisdom in the fear of EL with diligence; For
though there be a leading into captivity, and cities and
lands be destroyed, and gold and silver and every possession perish, the wisdom of the wise can no one take away,
excepf the blindness of ungodliness, and the callousness
(that comes) of sin.

For if one keep oneself from these evil things, Then
even among his enemies shall wisdom be a glory to him,
And in a strange country a fatherland, And in the midst of
foes shall prove a friend. Whosoever teaches noble things
and does them, shall be enthroned with kings, as was also
Joseph my brother.

Therefore, my children, I have learned that at the end
of the ages you will transgress against Yahua, stretching
out hands to wickedness [against Him]; and to all the
Gentiles shall you become a scorn. For our father Israel
is pure from the transgressions of the chief priests. For as
the heaven is purer in Yahua's sight than the earth, so also
be you, the lights of Israel, (purer) than all the Gentiles.

But if you be darkened through transgressions, what,
therefore, will all the Gentiles do living in blindness? Yes,
you shall bring a curse upon our race, because the light of
the law which was given for to lighten every man this you
desire to destroy by teaching commandments contrary to

the ordinances of EL. The offerings of Yahua you shall rob, and from His portion shall you steal choice portions, eating (them) contemptuously with harlots.

And out of covetousness you shall teach the commandments of Yahua. Married women shall you pollute, and the virgins of Jerusalem shall you defile: and with harlots and adulteresses shall you be joined, and the daughters of the Gentiles shall you take to wife, purifying them with an unlawful purification; and your union shall be like to Sodom and Gomorrah.

And you shall be puffed up because of your priesthood, lifting yourselves up against men, and not only so, but also against the commands of EL. For you shall contempt the holy things with jests and laughter.

Therefore the temple, which Yahua shall choose, shall be laid waste through your uncleanness, and you shall be captives throughout all nations. And you shall be an abomination to them, and you shall receive reproach and everlasting shame from the righteous judgement of EL. And all who hate you shall rejoice at your destruction. And if you were not to receive mercy through Abraham, Isaac, and Jacob, our fathers, not one of our seed should be left upon the earth.

And now I have learned that for seventy weeks you shall go astray, and profane the priesthood, and pollute the sacrifices. And you shall make void the law, and set at nought the words of the prophets by evil perverseness. And you shall persecute righteous men, and hate the godly and the words of the faithful shall you abhor. [And a man who renews the law in the power of the Most High, you shall call a deceiver; and at last you shall rush (upon him) to slay him, not knowing his dignity, taking innocent blood through wickedness upon your heads.] And your holy places shall be laid waste even to the ground because of him. And you shall have no place that is clean;

but you shall be among the gentiles a curse and a dispersion until He shall again visit you and in pity shall receive you.

And whereas you have heard concerning the seventy weeks, hear also concerning the priesthood. For in each jubilee there shall be a priesthood.

And in the first jubilee, the first who is anointed to the priesthood shall be great, and shall speak to EL as to a father. And his priesthood shall be perfect with Yahua.

In the second jubilee, he that is anointed shall be conceived in the sorrow of beloved ones; and his priesthood shall be honoured and shall be glorified by all.

And the third priest shall be taken hold of by sorrow.

And the fourth shall be in pain, because unrighteousness shall gather itself against him exceedingly, and all Israel shall hate each one his neighbour.

The fifth shall be taken hold of by darkness.

Likewise also the sixth and the seventh.

And in the seventh shall be such pollution as I cannot express before men for they shall know it who do these things. Therefore shall they be taken captive and become a prey, and their land and their substance shall be destroyed.

And in the fifth week they shall return to their desolate country, and shall renew the house of Yahua.

And in the seventh week shall become priests, (who are) idolaters, adulterers, lovers of money, proud, lawless, lascivious, abusers of children and beasts. And after their punishment shall have come from Yahua, the priesthood shall fail.

Then shall Yahua raise up a new priest. And to him all the words of Yahua shall be revealed; And he shall execute a righteous judgement upon the earth for a multitude of days. And his star shall arise in heaven as of a king. Lighting up the light of knowledge as the sun the day, And he shall be magnified in the world. He shall shine forth as the sun on the earth, And shall remove all darkness from under heaven, And there shall be peace in all the earth. The heavens shall exult in his days, And the earth shall be glad, And the clouds shall rejoice.

[And the knowledge of Yahua shall be poured forth upon the earth, as the water of the seas; And the Messengers of the glory of the presence of Yahua shall be glad in him. The heavens shall be opened, And from the temple of glory shall come upon him sanctification, with the Father's voice as from Abraham to Isaac. And the glory of the Most High shall be uttered over him, And the spirit of understanding and sanctification shall rest upon him. For he shall give the majesty of Yahua to His sons in truth for evermore; And there shall none succeed him for all generations for ever. And in his priesthood the Gentiles shall be multiplied in knowledge upon the earth, And enlightened through the grace of Yahua: In his priesthood shall sin come to an end, And the lawless shall cease to do evil. And he shall open the gates of paradise, And shall remove the threatening sword against Adam. And he shall give to the saints to eat from the tree of life, And the spirit of holiness shall be on them. And Beliar shall be bound by him, And he shall give power to His children to tread upon the evil spirits. And Yahua shall rejoice in His children, And be well pleased in His beloved ones for ever. Then shall Abraham and Isaac and Jacob exult, And I will be glad, And all the saints shall clothe themselves with joy.

And now, my children, you have heard all; therefore choose for yourselves either the light or the darkness, either the law of Yahua or the works of Beliar.

And his sons answered him, saying, "Before Yahua we will walk according to His law."

And their father said to them, "Yahua is witness, and His Messengers are witnesses, and you are witnesses, and

I am witness, concerning the word of your mouth."

And his sons said to him, "We are witnesses."

And thus Levi ceased commanding his sons; and he stretched out his feet on the bed, and was gathered to his fathers, after he had lived a hundred and thirty-seven years. And they laid him in a coffin, and afterwards they buried him in Hebron, with Abraham, Isaac, and Jacob

# The Testament of Judah

## The Fourth Son of Jacob and Leah

The copy of the words of Judah, what things he spake to his sons before he died. They gathered themselves together, therefore, and came to him, and he said to them:

Listen, my children, to Judah your father. I was the fourth son born to my father Jacob; and Leah my mother named me Judah, saying, "I give thanks to Yahua, because He hath given me a fourth son also."

I was swift in my youth, and obedient to my father in everything. And I honoured my mother and my mother's sister.

And it came to pass, when I became a man, that my father blessed me, saying, You shalt be a king, prospering in all things.

And Yahua showed me favour in all my works both in the field and in the house. I know that I raced a deer, and caught it, and prepared the meat for my father, which he ate. And the roes I used to master in the chase, and overtake all that was in the plains. A wild mare I overtook, and caught it and tamed it. I slew a lion and plucked a kid out of its mouth. I took a bear by its paw and hurled it down the cliff, and it was crushed. I outran the wild boar, and seizing it as I ran, I tore it in sunder. A leopard in Hebron leaped upon my dog, and I caught it by the tail, and hurled it on the rocks, and it was broken in twain. I found a wild ox feeding in the fields, and seizing it by the horns, and whirling it round and stunning it, I cast it from me and slew it.

And when the two kings of the Canaanites came sheathed in armor against our flocks, and many people with them, single-handed I rushed upon the king of Hazor, and smote him on the greaves and dragged him down, and so I Slew him.

And the other, the king of Tappuah, as he sat upon his horse, [I slew, and so I scattered all his people.]

Achor the king, a man of giant stature I found, hurling javelins before and behind as he sat on horseback, and I took up a stone of sixty pounds weight, and hurled it and smote his horse, and killed it. And I fought with Achor for two hours; and I cut his shield in two and chopped off his feet, and killed him.

And as I was stripping off his breastplate, nine men, his companions, began to fight with me. And I wound my garment on my hand; and I slung stones at them, and killed four of them, and the rest fled.

And Jacob my father slew Beelesath, king of all the kings, a giant in strength, twelve cubits high. And fear fell upon them, and they ceased warring against us. Therefore my father was free from anxiety in the wars when I was with my brothers. For he saw in a vision concerning me that an Messenger of might followed me everywhere, that I should not be overcome.

And in the south there came upon us a greater war than that in Shechem; and I joined in battle array with my brothers, and pursued a thousand men, and slew of them two hundred men and four kings. And I went up upon the wall, and I slew four mighty men. And so we captured Hazor, and took all the spoil.

On the next day we departed to Aretan, a city strong and walled and inaccessible, threatening us with death. But I and Gad approached on the east side of the city, and Reuben and Levi on the west. And they that were on the wall, thinking that we were alone, were drawn down against us. And so my brothers secretly climbed up the wall on both sides by stakes, and entered the city, unknown to the men. And we took it with the edge of the sword. And as for those who had taken refuge in the tower, we set fire to the tower and took both it and them.

And as we were departing the men of Tappuah set upon our spoil, and were delivering it up to their sons. We fought with them as far as Tappuah. And we slew them and burnt their city, and took as spoil all that was in it.

And when I was at the waters of Kozeba, the men of Jobel came against us to battle. And we fought with them and routed them; and their allies from Shiloh we slew, and we did not leave them power to come in against us.

And the men of Makir came upon us the fifth day, to seize our spoil; and we attacked them and overcame them in fierce battle: for there was a company of mighty men among them, and we slew them before they had gone up the ascent.

When we came to their city their women rolled stones upon us from the brow of the hill on which the city stood, But Simeon and I hid ourselves behind the town, and seized upon the heights, and destroyed this city also.

The next day it was told us that the king of the city of Gaash with a mighty army was coming against us. I, therefore, and Dan feigned ourselves to be Amorites, and, as "allies" we went into their city. And in the depth of night our brothers came and we opened the gates to them. And we destroyed all the men and their substance, and we took for a prey all that was theirs, and their three walls we cast down.

And we drew near to Thamna, where was all the substance of the hostile kings. Then being insulted by them, I was therefore angry, and rushed against them to the summit while they kept slinging against me stones and arrows. And had not Dan my brother aided me, they would have slain me. We came upon them, therefore, with anger, and they all fled, Then passing by another way, they besought my father, and he made peace with them. And we did to them no hurt, and they became tributary to us, and we restored to them their spoil. And I built Thamna, and my father built Pabael.

I was twenty years old when this war happend, and the Canaanites feared me and my brothers.

And I had much cattle, and I had for chief herdsman, Iram the Adullamite. And when I went to him I saw Parsaba, king of Adullam; and he spoke to us, and made us a feast. And when I was heated he gave me his daughter Bathshua to wife. She bare me Er, and Onan and Shelah; and two of them Yahua smote: for Shelah lived, and his children are you.

And eighteen years my father abode in peace with his brother Esau, and his sons with us, after that we came from Mesopotamia, from Laban.

And when eighteen years had passed, in the forties years of my life, Esau, the brother of my father, came upon us with a mighty and strong people. And Jacob smote Esau with an arrow, and he was taken up wounded on Mount Seir, and as he went he died at Anoniram.

And we pursued after the sons of Esau. Now they had a city with walls of iron and gates of brass; and we could not enter into it, and we encamped around, and besieged it. And when they did not opened to us in twenty days, I set up a ladder in the sight of all and with my shield upon my head I went up, sustaining the assault of stones upwards of three talents weight, and I slew four of their mighty men. And Reuben and Gad slew six others.

Then they asked from us terms of peace; and having taken counsel with our father, we received them as tributaries. And they gave us five hundred cors of wheat, five hundred baths of oil, five hundred measures of wine, until the famine, when we went down into Egypt.

And after these things my son Er took to wife Tamar, from Mesopotamia, a daughter of Aram. Now Er was wicked, and he was in need concerning Tamar, because she was not of the land of Canaan. And on the third night a Messenger of Yahua smote him. And he had not known her according to the evil craftiness of his mother, for he did not wish to have children by her.

In the days of the wedding-feast I gave Onan to her in marriage; and he also in wickedness knew her not, though he spent with her a year. And when I threatened him he went in to her, but he spilled his sperm on the ground, according to the command of his mother, and he also died through wickedness.

And I wished to give Shelah also to her, but his mother did not permit it; for she wrought evil against Tamar, because she was not of the daughters of Canaan, as she also herself was.

And I knew that the race of the Canaanites was wicked, but the impulse of youth blinded my mind. And when I saw her pouring out wine, owing to the intoxication of wine I was deceived, and took her although my father had not counselled (it).

And while I was away she went and took for Shelah a wife from Canaan. And when I knew what she had done, I cursed her in the anguish of my soul. And she also died through her wickedness together with her sons.

And after these things, while Tamar was a widow, she heard after two years that I was going up to shear my sheep, and adorned herself in bridal array, and sat in the city Enaim by the gate. For it was a law of the Amorites, that she who was about to marry should sit in fornication seven days by the gate.

Therefore being drunk with wine, I did not recognize her; and her beauty deceived me, through the fashion of her adorning. And I turned aside to her, and said, "Let me go in to you."

And she said, "What wilt you give me?"

And I gave her my staff, and my girdle, and the diadem of my kingdom in pledge. And I went in to her, and she conceived. And not knowing what I had done, I wished to slay her; but she privily sent my pledges, and put me to shame. And when I called her, I heard also the secret words which I spoke when lying with her in my drunkenness; and I could not slay her, because it was from Yahua. For I said, Lest haply she did it in subtlety, having received the pledge from another woman. But I came not again near her while I lived, because I had done this abomination in all Israel.

Moreover, they who were in the city said there was no harlot in the gate, because she came from another place, and sat for a while in the gate. And I thought that no one knew that I had gone in to her.

And after this we came into Egypt to Joseph, because of the famine. And I was forty and six years old, and seventy and three years lived I in Egypt.

And now I command you, my children, pay attention to Judah your father, and keep my sayings to perform all the ordinances of Yahua, and to obey the commands of EL. And do not walk after your lusts, nor in the imaginations of your thoughts in haughtiness of heart; and do not glory in the deeds and strength of your youth, for this also is evil in the eyes of Yahua.

Since I also gloried that in wars no comely woman's face ever enticed me, and reproved Reuben my brother concerning Bilhah, the wife of my father, the spirits of jealousy and of fornication arrayed themselves against me, until I lay with Bathshua the Canaanite, and Tamar, who was espoused to my sons. For I said to my father-in-law, "I will take counsel with my father, and so will I take your daughter."

But he was unwilling, and he showed me a boundless store of gold in his daughter's behalf; for he was a king. And he adorned her with gold and pearls, and caused her to pour out wine for us at the feast with the beauty of women. And the wine turned aside my eyes, and pleasure blinded my heart. And I became enamoured of her and I lay with her, and transgressed the commandment of the Yahua and the commandment of my fathers, and I took her to wife.

And Yahua rewarded me according to the imagination of my heart, inasmuch as I had no joy in her children.

And now, my children, I say to you, be not drunk with wine; for wine turnes the mind away from the truth, and inspires the passion of lust, and leads the eyes into error.

For the spirit of fornication has wine as a minister to give pleasure to the mind; for these two also take away the mind of man. For if a man drinks wine to drunkenness, it disturbes the mind with filthy thoughts leading to fornication, and heats the body to carnal union; and if the occasion of the lust be present, he workes the sin, and is not ashamed.

Such is the inebriated man, my children; for he who is drunken reverences no man. For, lo, it made me also to err, so that I was not ashamed of the multitude in the city, in that before the eyes of all I turned aside to Tamar, and I wrought a great sin, and I uncovered the covering of my sons' shame.

After I had drunk wine I did not revere the commandment of EL, and I took a woman of Canaan to wife. For much discretion is needed by the man who drinkes wine, my children. And herein is discretion in drinking wine: a man may drink so long as he preserves modesty. But if he go beyond this limit the spirit of deceit attacks his mind, and it makes the drunkard to talk filthily, and to transgress and not to be ashamed, but even to glory in his shame, and to account himself honourable.

He that committes fornication is not aware when he suffers loss, and is not ashamed when put to dishonour. For even though a man be a king and commit fornication, he is stripped of his kingship by becoming the slave of fornication, as I myself also suffered. For I gave my staff, that is, the stay of my tribe; and my girdle, that is, my power; and my diadem, that is, the glory of my kingdom.

And indeed I repented of these things; wine and flesh I did not eat until my old age, nor did I behold any joy.

And the Messenger of EL showed me that for ever do women bear rule over king and beggar alike. And from the king they take away his glory, and from the valiant man his might, and from the beggar even that little which is the stay of his poverty.

Observe, therefore, my children, the limit in wine; for there are in it four evil spirits--- of lust, of hot desire, of wasteful behavior, of filthy lucre.

If you drink wine in gladness, then you might become modest in the fear of EL. For if in (your) gladness the fear of EL departs, then drunkenness arises and shamelessness steals in.

But if you would live soberly do not touch wine at all, lest you sin in words of outrage, and in fightings and slanders, and transgressions of the commandments of EL, and you perish before your time.

Moreover, wine reveals the mysteries of EL and men, even as I also revealed the commandments of EL and the mysteries of Jacob my father to the Canaanitish woman Bathshua, which EL bade me not to reveal. And wine is a cause both of war and confusion.

And now, I command you, my children, not to love

money, nor to gaze upon the beauty of women; because for the sake of money and beauty I was led astray to Bathshua the Canaanite.

For I know that because of these two things shall my race fall into wickedness. For even wise men among my sons shall they mar, and shall cause the kingdom of Judah to be diminished, which Yahua gave me because of my obedience to my father. For I never caused grief to Jacob, my father. For all things he commanded I did.

And Isaac, the father of my father, blessed me to be king in Israel, and Jacob further blessed me in like manner. And I know that from me shall the kingdom be established.

And I know what evils you will do in the last days. Beware, therefore, my children, of fornication, and the love of money, and listen to Judah your father. For these things take you away from the law of EL, And blind the inclination of the soul,  teach arrogance, do not allow a man to have compassion upon his neighbor. They rob his soul of all goodness, and oppress him with toils and troubles, and drive away sleep from him, and devour his flesh. And he hindesr the sacrifices of EL; And he does not remember the blessing of EL, He does not hear and pay attention to a prophet when he speaks. He resents the words of godliness. For he is a slave to two contrary passions, And cannot obey EL, because they have blinded his soul, And he walkes in the day as in the night.

My children, the love of money leades to idolatry; because, when led astray through money, men name as gods those who are not Elohim, and it causes him who has it to fall into madness. For the sake of money I lost my children, and had not my repentance, and my humiliation, and the prayers of my father been accepted, I should have died childless. But the EL of my fathers had mercy on me, because I did it in ignorance. And the prince of deceit blinded me, and I sinned as a man and as flesh, being corrupted through sins; and I learned my own weakness while thinking myself invincible.

Know, therefore, my children, that two spirits wait upon man the spirit of truth and the spirit of deceit. And in the midst is the spirit of understanding of the mind, to which it belongs to turn whithersoever it will. And the works of truth and the works of deceit are written upon the hearts of men, and each one of them Yahua knows. And there is no time at which the works of men can be hid. For on the heart itself have they been written down before Yahua. And the spirit of truth testifies all things, and accuses all; and the sinner is burned up by his own heart, and cannot raise his face to the judge.

And now, my children, I command you, love Levi, that you may abide, and exalt not yourselves against him, lest you be utterly destroyed.

For to me Yahua gave the kingdom, and to him the priesthood, and He set the kingdom beneath the priesthood. To me He gave the things upon the earth; to him the things in the heavens. As the heaven is higher than the earth, so is the priesthood of EL higher than the earthly kingdom, unless it falls away through sin from Yahua and is dominated by the earthly kingdom. For the Messenger of Yahua said to me: "Yahua chose him rather than you, to draw near to Him, and to eat of His table and to offer Him the first-fruits of the choice things of the sons of Israel; but you shalt be king of Jacob. And you shalt be among them as the sea. For as, on the sea, just and unjust are tossed about, some taken into captivity while some are enriched, so also shall every race of men be in you: some shall be impoverished, being taken captive, and others grow rich by plundering the possessions of others. For the kings shall be as sea-monsters. They shall swallow men like fishes. The sons and daughters of free men they shall enslave. Houses, lands, flocks, money they shall plunder. And with the flesh of many they shall wrongfully feed the ravens and the cranes. They shall advance in evil, in covetousness uplifted, And there shall be false prophets like tempests, and they shall persecute all righteous men.

"And Yahua shall bring upon them divisions one against another. And there shall be continual wars in Israel. And among men of another race shall my kingdom be brought to an end until the salvation of Israel shall come, until the appearing of the EL of righteousness, That Jacob may rest in peace. "

And He shall guard the might of my kingdom for ever; For Yahua sware to me with an oath that He would not destroy the kingdom from my seed for ever.

Now I have much grief, my children, because of your lewdness and witchcrafts, and idolatries which you shall practice against the kingdom, following them that have familiar spirits, diviners, and demons of error. You shall make your daughters singing girls and harlots, and you shall mingle in the abominations of the gentiles. For which things' sake Yahua shall bring upon you famine and pestilence, death and the sword, the beleaguering by enemies, the revilings of friends, the slaughter of children, the rape of wives, the plundering of possessions, the burning of the temple of EL,the laying waste of the land, the enslavement of yourselves among the gentiles. And they shall make some of you eunuchs for their wives. Until Yahua visit you, when with perfect heart you repent and walk in all His commandments, and He bring you up from captivity among the gentiles.

And after these things shall a star arise to you from Jacob in peace, And a man shall arise, like the sun of righteousness, walking with the sons of men in meekness and righteousness. And no sin shall be found in him. and the heavens shall be open to him, to pour out the spirit, the blessing of EL. And He shall pour out the spirit of grace upon you, and you shall be to Him sons in truth. And you shall walk in His commandments first and last. Then shall the sceptre of my kingdom shine forth, and from your root shall arise a stem, and from it shall grow a rod of righteousness to the gentiles, to judge and to save all that call upon Yahua.

And after these things shall Abraham and Isaac and Jacob arise to life, and I and my brothers shall be chiefs of the tribes of Israel: Levi first, I the second, Joseph third, Benjamin fourth, Simeon fifth; Issachar sixth, and so all in order.

And Yahua blessed Levi, and the Messenger of the Presence, me; the powers of glory, Simeon; the heaven, Reuben; the earth, Issachar; the sea, Zebulun; the mountains, Joseph; the tabernacle, Benjamin; the luminaries, Dan; Eden, Naphtali; the sun, Gad; the moon, Asher.

And you shall be the people of Yahua, and have one tongue; And there shall be there no spirit of deceit of Beliar. For he shall be cast into the fire for ever. And they who have died in grief shall arise in joy. And they who were poor for Yahua's sake shall be made rich. And they who are put to death for Yahua's sake shall awake to life.

And the harts of Jacob shall run in joyfulness, And the eagles of Israel shall fly in gladness; And all the people shall glorify Yahua for ever.

Observe, therefore, my children, all the law of Yahua, for there is hope for all them who hold fast to His ways.

And he said to them, "Behold, I die before your eyes this day, a hundred and nineteen years old. Let no one bury me in costly apparel, nor tear open my bowels, for this shall they who are kings do; and carry me up to Hebron with you."

And Judah, when he had said these things, fell asleep; and his sons did according to all whatsoever he commanded them, and they buried him in Hebron, with his fathers.

# The Testament of Issachar

## The Fifth Son of Jacob and Leah

The copy of the words of Issachar. For he called his sons and said to them:

Pay attention, my children, to Issachar your father. Listen to the words of him who is beloved of Yahua.

I was born the fifth son to Jacob by way of hire for the mandrakes. For Reuben my brother brought in mandrakes from the field, and Rachel met him and took them. And Reuben wept, and at his voice Leah my mother came.

Now these (mandrakes) were sweet-smelling apples. which were produced in the land of Haran below a ravine of water. And Rachel said, "I will not give them to you, but they shall be to me instead of children. For Yahua has despised me, and I have not born children to Jacob."

Now there were two apples; and Leah said to Rachel: "Let it satisfy you that you have taken my husband. Will you take these also?"

And Rachel said to her, "You shall have Jacob this night for the mandrakes of your son."

And Leah said to her, "Jacob is mine for I am the wife of his youth."

But Rachel said "Do not boast and puff up yourself yourself for he espoused me before you, and for my sake he served our father fourteen years. And had not craft increased on the earth and the wickedness of men prospered, you would not now see the face of Jacob."

Then a Messenger of Yahua appeared to Jacob, saying, "Two children shall Rachel bear inasmuch as she has refused company with her husband and has chosen continency."

And had not Leah my mother paid the two apples for the sake of his company, she would have borne eight sons. for this reason she bare six, and Rachel bare the two. For on account of the mandrakes Yahua visited her. For He knew that for the sake of children she wished to company with Jacob, and not for lust of pleasure. For on the morrow also she again gave up Jacob because of the mandrakes. Therefore, Yahua paid attention to Rachel. For though she desired them, she did not eat them, but offered them in the house of Yahua, presenting them to the priest of the Most High who was at that time.

When, therefore, I grew up, my children, I walked in uprightness of heart, and I became a husbandman for my father and my brothers, and I brought in fruits from the field according to their season. And my father blessed me, for he saw that I walked in rectitude before him. And I was not a busybody in my doings, nor envious and malicious against my neighbour. I never slandered any one, nor did I censure the life of any man, walking as I did in singleness of eye.

Therefore, when I was thirty-five years old, I took to myself a wife for my labour wore away my strength, and I never thought upon pleasure with women. Because of my toil, sleep overcame me.

And my father always rejoiced in my rectitude, because I offered through the priest to Yahua all first-fruits, and then to my father also. And Yahua increased ten thousandfold His benefits in my hands; and also Jacob, my father, knew that EL aided my singleness. For on all the poor and oppressed I bestowed the good things of the earth in the singleness of my heart.

And now, listen to me, my children, and walk in singleness of your heart, For I have seen in it all that is well-pleasing to Yahua. The single-(minded) man does not covet gold. He does not overreach his neighbor, He does not long after many dainties. He does not delight in varied apparel. He does not desire to live a long life, but only waits for the will of EL. The spirits of deceit have no power against him. For he does not look longingly on the beauty of women, lest he should pollute his mind with corruption. There is no envy in his thoughts, nor worry with insatiable desire in his mind. For he walk in single-ness of soul, And behold all things in uprightness of heart, Shunning eyes (made) evil through the error of the world, lest he should see the perversion of any of the command-ments of Yahua.

Therefore, my children, keep the law of EL. And get singleness. And walk in guilelessness, Not playing the busybody with the business of your neighbor. But love Yahua and your neighbor. Have compassion on the poor and weak. Bow down your back to husbandry. And toil in labors in all manner of husbandry, offering gifts to Yahua with thanksgiving. For with the first-fruits of the earth will Yahua bless you, even as He blessed all the saints from Abel even until now.

For no other portion is given to you than of the fatness of the earth, whose fruits are raised by toil. For our father Jacob blessed me with blessings of the earth and of first-fruits.

And Levi and Judah were glorified by Yahua even among the sons of Jacob. For Yahua gave them an inheri-tance. To Levi He gave the priesthood, and to Judah the kingdom. And do you therefore obey them, and walk in the singleness of your father.

Therefore, know this, my children, that in the last times your sons will forsake singleness, and will cleave to insatiable desire. And leaving guilelessness will draw near to malice. Forsaking the commandments of Yahua, they will cleave to Beliar. And leaving husbandry, they will follow after their own wicked devices. They shall be dispersed among the Gentiles and shall serve their enemies. Therefore give these commands to your children, that, if they sin, they may the more quickly return to Yahua. For He is merciful, and will deliver them, even to bring them back into their land.

Look and see, I am a hundred and twenty-six years old and am not conscious of committing any sin. Except for my wife I have not known any woman. I never committed fornication by the gaze of my eyes. I did not drink, to be led astray by it. I did not covet any desirable thing that was my neighbor's. Guile did not arise not in my heart. A lie did not pass through my lips. If any man were in distress I joined my sighs with his. And I shared my bread with the poor. I produced godliness all my days, and I kept truth. I loved Yahua, and likewise also every man with all my heart.

So do you also these things, my children, And every spirit of Beliar shall flee from you, And no deed of wicked men shall rule over you; And every wild beast shall you subdue because you have with you the EL of heaven and earth and walk with men in singleness of heart.

And having said these things, he commanded his sons that they should carry him up to Hebron, and bury him there in the cave with his fathers. And he stretched out his feet and died, at a good old age; with every limb sound, and with strength unabated, he slept the eternal sleep.

# The Testament of Zebulun

## The Sixth Son of Jacob and Leah

T he copy of the words of Zebulun, which he enjoined on his sons before he died in the hundred and fourteenth year of his life, two years after the death of Joseph. And he said to them:

Pay attention to me, you sons of Zebulun, attend to the words of your father. I, Zebulun, was born a good gift to my parents. For when I was born my father was increased very exceedingly, both in flocks and herds, when with the straked rods he had his portion.

I am not conscious that I have sinned all my days, save in thought. Nor yet do I remember that I have done any iniquity, except the sin of ignorance which I committed against Joseph. For I made an agreement with my brothers not to tell my father what had been done. But I wept in secret many days on account of Joseph, for I feared my brothers because they had all agreed that if any one should tell the secret, he should be killed. But when they wished to kill Joseph, I begged them with much tears not to be guilty of this sin.

For Simeon and Gad came against Joseph to kill him, and he said to them with tears, "Pity me, my brothers, have mercy upon the bowels of Jacob our father. Do not lay your hands upon me to shed innocent blood, for I have not sinned against you. And if indeed I have sinned, chastise me, my brothers but do not lay your hand upon me for the sake of Jacob our father."

And as he spoke these words, wailing as he did so, I

was unable to bear his lamentations, and began to weep, and my liver was poured out, and all the substance of my bowels was loosened. And I wept with Joseph, and my heart sounded, and the joints of my body trembled, and I was not able to stand.

And when Joseph saw me weeping with him and them coming against him to slay him, he fled behind me, pleading with them.

But meanwhile Reuben arose and said: "Come, my brothers, let us not kill him, but let us cast him into one of these dry pits, which our fathers digged and found no water."

For for this cause Yahua forbade that water should rise up in them in order that Joseph should be preserved. And they did so until they sold him to the Ishmaelites.

For in his price I had no share, my children. But Simeon and Gad and six others of our brothers took the price of Joseph, and bought sandals for themselves, and their wives, and their children, saying, "We will not eat of it, for it is the price of our brother's blood, but we will as-suredly tread it under foot, because he said that he would be king over us, and so let us see what will become of his dreams."

[Scribe's additions: Therefore it is written in the writing of the law of Moses, that whosoever will not raise up seed to his brother, his sandal should be unloosed, and they should spit in his face.

And the brothers of Joseph did not wish that their brother should live, and Yahua loosed from them the sandal, which they wore against Joseph their brother. For when they came into Egypt they were unloosed by the servants of Joseph outside the gate, and so they pledged obedience to Joseph after the fashion of King Pharaoh.

And not only did they make obeisance to him, but were spit upon also, falling down before him forthwith, and so they were put to shame before the Egyptians. For after this the Egyptians heard all the evils that they had done to Joseph. ]

And after he was sold my brothers sat down to eat and drink. But I, through pity for Joseph, did not eat, but watched the pit, since Judah feared lest Simeon, Dan, and Gad should rush off and slay him. But when they saw that I did not eat, they set me to watch him, till he was sold to the Ishmaelites.

And when Reuben came and heard that while he was away (Joseph) had been sold, he tore his garments, (and) mourning, said, "How shall I look on the face of my father Jacob?"

And he took the money and ran after the merchants, but as he failed to find them he returned grieving. But the merchants had left the broad road and marched through the Troglodytes by a short cut. But Reuben was grieved, and ate no food that day.

So Dan came to him and said. "Do not weep, neither grieve; for we have found what we can say to our father Jacob. Let us slay a kid of the goats, and dip in it the coat of Joseph. Then let us send it to Jacob, saying, 'Do you know? Is this the coat of thy son? "

And they did so. For they stripped the coat off from Joseph when they were selling him, and put upon him the garment of a slave. Now Simeon took the coat, and would not give it up, for he wished to rend it with his sword, as he was angry that Joseph lived and that he had not slain him. Then we all rose up and said to him: "If you do not gives up the coat, we 13 will say to our father that you alone didst this evil thing in Israel."

And so he gave it to them, and they did even as Dan had said.

And now, my children, I bid you to keep the commands of Yahua, and to show mercy to your neighbors, and to have compassion towards all, not towards men only, but also towards, beasts. For all this thing's sake Yahua blessed me, and when all my brothers were sick, I escaped without sickness, for Yahua knowes the purposes of each. Have, therefore, compassion in your hearts, my children, because even as a man does to his neighbor even so also will Yahua do to him. For the sons of my brothers were sickening and were dying on account of Joseph, because they showed no mercy in their hearts; but my sons were preserved without sickness, as you know. And when I was in the land of Canaan, by the sea-coast, I made a catch of fish for Jacob my father; and when many were choked in the sea, I continued unhurt.

I was the first to make a boat to sail upon the sea, for Yahua gave me understanding and wisdom about this. And I let down a rudder behind it, and I stretched a sail upon another upright piece of wood in the middle. And I sailed in the boat along the shores, catching fish for the house of my father until we came to Egypt. For five years I caught fish. In the summer I caught fish, and in the winter I kept sheep with my brothers.

[Scribe's additions: And through compassion I shared my catch with every stranger. And if a man were a stranger, or sick, or aged, I boiled the fish, and dressed them well, and offered them to all men, as every man had need, grieving with and having compassion upon them. On this account also Yahua satisfied me with abundance of fish when catching fish. For he that shares with his neighbor receives many times more from Yahua.

Now I will declare to you what I did. I saw a man in distress through nakedness in winter time, and had compassion upon him, and stole away a garment secretly from my father's house, and gave it to him who was in distress. Do you, therefore, my children, from that which EL bestowes upon you, show compassion and mercy without hesitation to all men, and give to every man with a good heart. And if you have not the wherewithal to give to him that needs, have compassion for him in bowels of mercy. I know that my hand found not the wherewithal to give to him that needed, and I walked with him weeping for seven furlongs, and my bowels yearned towards him in compassion.

Have, therefore, yourselves also, my children, compassion towards every man with mercy, that Yahua also may have compassion and mercy upon you.

Because also in the last days, EL will send His compassion on the earth, and wheresoever He find bowels of mercy He dwell in him. For in the degree in which a man hath compassion upon his neighbors, in the same degree hath the Yahua also upon him.]

And when we went down into Egypt, Joseph bore no malice against us. To whom taking heed, do you also, my children, approve yourselves without malice, and love one another; and do not set down in account, each one of you, evil against his brother. For this break unity and divides all kindred, and troubles the soul, and wear away the countenance.

Observe, therefore, the waters, and know when they flow together, they sweep along stones, trees, earth, and other things. But if they are divided into many streams, the earth swallow them up, and they vanish away. So shall you also be if you are divided.

Therefore, do not be divided into two heads, for everything which Yahua made has but one head, and two shoulders, two hands, two feet, and all the remaining members. For I have learned in the writing of my fathers, that You shall be divided in Israel, And you shall follow two kings, And shall work every abomination. And your enemies shall lead you captive, And you shall be evil entreated among the gentiles, With many infirmities and tribulations.

And after these things you shall remember Yahua, and repent,  for He is merciful and compassionate. And He sets not down in account evil to the sons of men, because they are flesh, And the spirits of deceit deceive them in all their deeds.

And after these things there shall arise to you Yahua Himself, the light of righteousness.  And he shall bring back all the gentiles into zeal for Him. And you shall return to your land. And you shall see Him in Jerusalem, for His name's sake.

And again through the wickedness of your works shall you provoke Him to anger, and you shall be cast away by

Him to the time of consummation.

And now, my children, do not grieve that I am dying, nor be cast down in that I am coming to my end. For I shall rise again in the midst of you, as a ruler in the midst of his sons; and I shall rejoice in the midst of my tribe, as many as shall keep the law of Yahua, and the commandments of Zebulun their father. But upon the ungodly shall Yahua bring eternal fire, and destroy them throughout all generations. But I am now hastening away to my rest, as did also my fathers. But fear Yahua our EL with all your strength all the days of your life.

And when he had said these things he fell asleep, at a good old age. And his sons laid him in a wooden coffin. And afterwards they carried him up and buried him in Hebron, with his fathers.

# The Testament of Dan

## The Seventh Son of Jacob and Bilhah

T he copy of the words of Dan, which he spake to his sons in his last days, in the hundred and twenty-fifth year of his life. For he called together his family, and said:

Listen carefully to my words, you sons of Dan; and give heed to the words of your father. I have proved in my heart, and in my whole life, that truth with just dealing is good and well pleasing to EL, and that lying and anger are evil, because they teach man all wickedness.

I confess, therefore, this day to you, my children, that in my heart I resolved on the death of Joseph my brother, the true and good man. [And I rejoiced that he was sold, because his father loved him more than us.] For the spirit of jealousy and vainglory said to me, "You yourself also are his son." And one of the spirits of Beliar stirred me up, saying, "Take this sword, and with it kill Joseph so that your father love you more when he is dead."

Now this is the spirit of anger that persuaded me to crush Joseph as a leopard crushes a kid. But the EL of my fathers did not suffer him to fall into my hands, so that I should find him alone and kill him, and cause a second tribe to be destroyed in Israel.

And now, my children, Look, I am dying, and I tell you the truth that unless you keep yourselves from the spirit of lying and of anger, and love truth and longsuffering, you shall perish. For anger is blindness and does not allow one to see the face of any man with truth.

For though it be a father or a mother, he behaves towards them as enemies. Though it be a brother, he does not know him. And though it be a prophet of Yahua, he disobeyes him. Though a righteous man, he does not regard him. Though a friend, he does not acknowledge him.

For the spirit of anger encompasses him with the net of deceit and blindes his eyes. And through lying darkens his mind, and gives him its own peculiar vision.

And what encompasses it his eyes? A heart of hatred, and he becomes envious of his brother.

For anger is an evil thing, my children, for it troubles even the soul itself. And it takes control of the body of the angry man and it makes its own. And it becomes the master over his life. It bestowes upon the body power so that it may work all iniquity. And when the body does all these things, the heart justifies what is done because it does not see aright.

Therefore he that is full of anger, if he is a mighty man, has three-times the power in his anger:

one by the help of his servants;

and a second by his wealth whereby he persuades and overcomes wrongfully;

and thirdly, having his own natural power he works the evil.

And though the wrathful man be weak, yet he has power that is two-times that which is by nature for wrath ever helps him in lawlessness. This spirit accompanies lying at the right hand of Satan that with cruelty and lying his works may be done.

Therefore, understand the power of wrath that it is vain. For it first of all it provodes through word. Then by works it strengthenes he who is angry. And with sharp losses disturbs his mind and then stirs up with great wrath his heart.

Therefore, when any one speaks against you, do not

be moved to anger. For first it pleases the one who hears the anger, and so makes the mind keen to perceive the grounds for further provocation. And then, being enraged, he thinks that his anger is justified.

If you fall into any loss or ruin, my children, do not afflicted. For this very spirit creates a desire for that which is perishable, in order to furhter enrage you through the affliction.

And if you suffer loss voluntarily or involuntarily do not be vexed because from vexation comes wrath with lying.

Moreover, wrath with lying is a twofold mischief because they assist one another in order to disturb the heart. Then when the heart is continually disturbed, Yahua departs from it, and Beliar rules over it.

Therefore, my children, pay attention to the commandments of Yahua, and keep His Instructions. Depart from wrath and hate lying, so that Yahua may dwell among you, and Beliar may flee from you.

Speak truth each one with his neighbour so that you shall not fall into wrath and confusion, but you shall be in peace, and having the EL of peace no war shall prevail over you.

Love Yahua through all your life, and love one another with a true heart.

I know that in the last days you shall depart from Yahua, and you shall provoke Levi to anger, and fight against Judah. But you shall not prevail against them because an Messenger of Yahua shall guide them both for by them shall Israel stand.

And whenever you depart from Yahua, you shall walk in all evil and work the abominations of the Gentiles, going a-whoring after women of the lawless ones, while the spirits of wickedness work in you. Therefore shall you be led away [with them] into captivity, and there you shall receive all the plagues of Egypt and all the evils of the Gentiles.

But when you return to Yahua you shall obtain mercy, and He shall bring you into His sanctuary, and He shall give you peace. And there shall arise to you from the tribe of Levi the salvation of Yahua, and he shall make war against Beliar, and execute an everlasting vengeance on our enemies. And he shall take the captives from Beliar, and turn disobedient hearts to Yahua, and give to them that call upon him eternal peace.

And the saints shall rest in Eden, and in the New Jerusalem shall the righteous rejoice, And it shall be to the glory of EL for ever. No longer shall Jerusalem endure desolation, nor Israel be led captive. For Yahua shall be in the midst of it, and the Holy One of Israel shall reign over it.

And now, fear Yahua, my children, and beware of Satan and his spirits. Draw near to EL and to the Messenger that intercedes for you, for he is a mediator between EL and man, and for the peace of Israel he shall stand up against the kingdom of the enemy. That is why the enemy is eager to destroy all that call upon Yahua, for he knows that on the day when which Israel shall repent, the kingdom of the enemy shall be brought to an end.

The very Messenger of peace shall strengthen Israel so that it will not fall into the extremity of evil. And it shall be in the time of the lawlessness of Israel that Yahua will not depart from them but will transform them into a nation that does His will. For none of the Messengers will be equal to him. And His name shall be in every place in Israel and among the Gentiles.

Therefore, my children, keep yourselves from every evil work and cast away wrath and all lying, Love truth and long-suffering.

And the things which you have heard from your father,

you also teach to your children. Depart, therefore, from all unrighteousness, and cleave to the righteousness of EL, and your descendants will be saved for ever.

And bury me near my fathers.

And when he had said these things he kissed them, and fell asleep at a good old age. And his sons buried him, and after that they carried up his bones and placed them near Abraham, and Isaac, and Jacob.

# The Testament of Naphtali

## The Eighth Son of Jacob and Bilhah

The copy of the testament of Naphtali, which he ordained at the time of his death in the hundred and thirties years of his life. When his sons were gathered together in the seventh month, on the first day of the month, while still in good health, he made them a feast of food and wine. And after he was awake in the morning, he said to them, "I am dying." And they did not believe him. And as he glorified Yahua, he grew strong and reminded them that after yesterday's feast he said he should die, and then he began to say:

Hear, my children, you sons of Naphtali, hear the words of your father. I was born from Bilhah, and because Rachel dealt craftily, and gave Bilhah in place of herself to Jacob, and she conceived and bare me upon Rachel's knees, therefore she called my name Naphtali.

For Rachel loved me very much because I was born upon her lap; and when I was still young she was desired to kiss me and say, "May I have a brother for you from my own womb just like you." And so Joseph was like me in all things, according to these prayers of Rachel.

Now my mother was Bilhah, daughter of Rotheus the brother of Deborah, Rebecca's nurse, who was born on the self-same day as Rachel. Rotheus was of the family of Abraham, a Chaldean. He feared EL, and was free-born and noble. He was taken captive and was bought by Laban, and he gave him Euna his handmaid to wife, and she bore a daughter and called her name Zilpah after the name of the village in which he had been taken captive.

And next she bore Bilhah, saying, "My daughter hastens after what is new." For immediately that she was born she seized the breast and hastened to suck it.

I was swift on my feet like the deer, and my father Jacob appointed me for all messages, and as a deer he gave me his blessing. For as the potter knows the vessel, how much it is to contain, and crafts the clay accordingly, so also does Yahua make the body after the likeness of the spirit, and according to the capacity of the body does He implant the spirit. And the one does not fall short of the other by a third part of a hair; for by weight, and measure, and rule was all the creation made.

And as the potter knows the use of each vessel, what it is suited for, so also does Yahua know the body, how far it will persist in goodness, and when it begins in evil. For there is no inclination or thought which Yahua does not know for He created every man after His own image.

As a man's strength, so also is his work; and as his mind, so also is his skill, and as his purpose, so also is his achievement; and as his heart, so also is his mouth; as his eye, so also is his sleep; as his soul, so also is his word, either in the law of Yahua or in the works of Beliar.

And as there is a division between light and darkness, between seeing and hearing, so also is there a division between man and man, and between woman and woman. And no one should say that the one is like the other either in face or in mind.

For EL made all things good in their order, the five senses in the head, and He joined on the neck to the head, adding to it the hair also for comeliness and glory, then the heart for understanding, the belly for excrement, and the stomach for (digestion), the windpipe for breathing, the liver for wrath, the gall for bitterness, the spleen for laughter, the reins for prudence, the muscles of the loins for power, the lungs for drawing in, the loins for strength, and so forth.

So then, my children, let all your works be done in order with good intent in the fear of EL, and do nothing disorderly in scorn or out of its due season. For if you bid the eye to hear, it cannot; so neither while you are in darkness can you do the works of light.

Therefore, do not be eager to corrupt your doings through covetousness or with vain words to beguile your souls because if you keep silence in purity of heart, you shall understand how to hold fast the will of EL, and to cast away the will of Beliar.

Sun and moon and stars do not change their order. So with you: do not also change the law of EL in the disorderliness of your doings. The Gentiles went astray and forsook Yahua and changed their order and obeyed sticks and stones and spirits of deceit.

But it shall not be so with you, my children, if you recognize in the heavens, in the earth, and in the sea, and in all created things, that Yahua made all things. Do not become as Sodom, which changed the order of nature. In like manner the Watchers also changed the order of their nature, whom Yahua cursed at the flood, on whose account He made the earth without inhabitants and fruitless.

These things I say to you, my children, for I have read in the writings of Enoch that you yourselves also shall depart from Yahua, walking according to all the lawlessness of the Gentiles, and you shall do according to all the wickedness of Sodom.

And Yahua shall bring captivity upon you, and there shall you serve your enemies, and you shall be bowed down with every affliction and tribulation, until Yahua have consumed you all. And after you have become diminished and made few, you shall return and acknowledge Yahua your EL, and He shall bring you back into your land according to His abundant mercy.

And it shall be, that after that they come into the land of their fathers, they shall again forget Yahua and become wicked.

And Yahua shall scatter them upon the face of all the earth, until the compassion of Yahua shall come, a man working righteousness and working mercy to all them that are afar off, and to them that are near.

For in the forties year of my life, I saw a vision on the Mount of Olives, on the east of Jerusalem, that the sun and the moon were standing still. And behold Isaac, the father of my father, said to us, "Run and lay hold of them, each one according to his strength; and to him that seizes them will the sun and moon belong."

And we all of us ran together, and Levi laid hold of the sun, and Judah out ran the others and seized the moon, and they were both of them lifted up with them.

And when Levi became as a sun, lo, a certain young man gave to him twelve branches of palm. And Judah was bright as the moon, and under their feet were twelve rays. [And the two, Levi and Judah, ran, and laid hold of them.] And, a bull upon the earth, with two great horns, and an eagle's wings upon its back; and we wished to seize him; but could not.

But Joseph came, and seized him, and ascended up with him on high. And I saw, for I was there, and behold a holy writing appeared to us, saying: Assyrians, Medes, Persians, Syrians, shall possess in captivity the twelve tribes of Israel.

And again, after seven days, I saw our father Jacob standing by the sea of Jamnia, and we were with him. And behold, there came a ship sailing by, without sailors or pilot; and there was written upon the ship, "The Ship of Jacob."

And our father said to us, "Come, let us embark on our ship."

And when he had gone on board, there arose a violent storm, and a mighty tempest of wind; and our father, who was holding the helm, departed from us. And we, being tossed with the tempest, were borne along over the sea; and the ship was filled with water, (and was) pounded by mighty waves until it was broken up.

And Joseph fled away upon a little boat, and we were all divided upon nine planks, and Levi and Judah were together. And we were all scattered to the ends of the earth. Then Levi, girt about with sackcloth, prayed for us all to Yahua. And when the storm ceased, the ship reached the land as it were in peace. And, our father came, and we all rejoiced together.

These two dreams I told to my father; and he said to me, "These things must be fulfilled in their season after Israel has endured many things."

Then my father said to me, "I believe EL that Joseph lives, for I see always that Yahua numbers him with you, " and he said, weeping, "Ah me, my son Joseph, you live, though I do not see you, and you do not see Jacob that begat you."

He caused me also to weep by these words, and I burned in my heart to declare that Joseph had been sold, but I feared my brorhwea.

And Look! my children, I have shown to you the last times, how everything shall come to pass in Israel. You also, therefore, charge your children that they be united to Levi and to Judah. For through them shall salvation arise to Israel, and in them shall Jacob be blessed. For through their tribes shall EL appear on earth to save the race of Israel and to gather together the righteous from amongst the Gentiles.

If you work that which is good, my children, both men

and Messengers shall bless you. And EL shall be glorified among the Gentiles through you, and the devil shall flee from you, and the wild beasts shall fear you, and Yahua shall love you.

As a man who has trained a child well is kept in kindly remembrance, so also for a good work there is a good remembrance before EL.

But he that does not do that which is good, both Messengers and men shall curse, and EL shall be dishonoured among the Gentiles through him, and the devil shall make him as his own peculiar instrumenta, and every wild beast shall master him, and Yahua shall hate him.

For the commandments of the law are twofold, and through prudence they must be fulfilled. For there is a season for a man to embrace his wife, and a season to abstain from embracing for his prayer. So, then, there are two commandments, and, unless they be done in due order, they bring very great sin upon men. So also is it with the other commandments.

Therefore, you be wise in EL, my Children, and prudent, understanding the order of His commandments, and the laws of every word, that Yahua may love you.

And when he had charged them with many such words, he exhorted them that they should remove his bones to Hebron, and that they should bury him with his fathers. And when he had eaten and drunken with a merry heart, he covered his face and died. And his sons did according to all that Naphtali their father had commanded them.

# The Testament of Gad

## The Ninth Son of Jacob and Zilpah

T he copy of the testament of Gad, what things he spake to his sons, in the hundred and twenty fifth year of his life, saying to them:

Listen to me, my children, I was the ninth son born to Jacob, and I was valiant in keeping the flocks. Accordingly I guarded at night the flock; and whenever a lion came, or the wolf, or any wild beast against the fold, I pursued it, and overtaking it I seized its foot with my hand and hurled it about a stone's throw, and so killed it.

Now Joseph my brother was feeding the flock with us for upwards of thirty days, and being young, he fell sick because of the heat. And he returned to Hebron to our father, who made him lie down near him because he loved him greatly. And Joseph told our father that the sons of Zilpah and Bilhah were slaying the best of the flock and eating them against the judgment of Reuben and Judah.

For he saw that I had delivered a lamb out of the mouth of a bear and put the bear to death, but I had slain the lamb because I was grieved concerning it that it could not live, and so we had eaten it.

And regarding this matter I was angry with Joseph until the day that he was sold, and the spirit of hatred was in me, and I wished not either to hear of Joseph with the ears, or see him with the eyes because he rebuked us to our faces saying that we, except Judah, were eating of the flock. For whatever things he told our father, he believed him.

I confess now my sin, my children, that oftentimes I wished to kill him, because I hated him from my heart.

Moreover, I hated him even more for his dreams; and I wished to lick him out of the land of the living, just like an ox licks up the grass of the field. Therefore Simeon and I sold him to the Ishmaelites. And thus through covetousness we were bent on slaying him. but the EL of my fathers delivered him from my hands, that I should not work lawlessness in Israel.

And now, my children, pay attention to the words of truth to work righteousness, and do all the law of the Most High, and do not go astray through the spirit of hatred, for it is evil in all the doings of men. Whatsoever a man does the hater abominates him. And though a man works the law of Yahua, He praises him not, and though a man fears Yahua and takes pleasure in that which is righteous. Yahua does not love him because this man disparages the truth, and envies those that prosper. He welcomes evil-speaking. He loves arrogance because hatred blinds his soul. Following this way I looked on Joseph.

Beware, therefore, my children of hatred for it works lawlessness even against Yahua Himself. For it will not hear the words of His commandments concerning the loving of one's neighbour, and it sins against EL. For if a brother stumble, hatred delights immediately to proclaim it to all men, and is urgent that he should be judged for it, and be punished and be put to death. And if it be a servant, hatred stirs him up against his master, and with every affliction it devises against him so that if possible he can be put to death.

For hatred works with envy also against them that prosper. So long as hatred hears of or sees their success, it always languishes with envy. For as love would quicken even the dead, and would call back them that are condemned to die, so hatred would slay the living, and even those that had sinned trivially it would not allow to live. For the spirit of hatred works together with Satan through hastiness of spirit in all things to men's death. But the spirit of love works together with the law of EL in long-suffering to the salvation of men.

Hatred, therefore, is evil, for it constantly mates with lying, speaking against the truth; and it makes small things to be great, and causes the light to be darkness, and calls the sweet bitter, and teaches slander, and kindles wrath, and stirs up war, and violence and all covetousness. It fills the heart with evils and devilish poison.

Therefore, These things I say to you from experience, my children, so that you may drive hatred from you. Hatrid is of the devil, and you should cleave to the love of EL.

Righteousness casts out hatred, and humility destroys envy. For he that is just and humble is ashamed to do what is unjust, being reproved not of another, but of his own heart because Yahua looks on his inclination. He does not speak not against a holy man because the fear of EL overcomes hatred. Fearing lest he should offend Yahua, he will not do wrong to any man - even in thought.

These things I learned at last, after I had repented concerning Joseph. For true repentance destroys ignorance, and] drives away the darkness, and enlightens the eyes, and gives knowledge to the soul, and leads the mind to salvation.

And those things which it hath not learned from man, it knows through repentance. For EL brought upon me a disease of the liver; and had not the prayers of Jacob my father helped and comforted me, it had hardly failed because my spirit had departed.

For by what things a man transgresses, by the same also is he punished. Since, therefore, my liver was set mercilessly against Joseph, in my liver too I suffered mercilessly and was judged for eleven months, for as long a time as I had been angry against Joseph.

And now, my children, I exhort you: each of you love your brother, and put away hatred from your hearts. Love one another in deed, in word, and in the inclination of the heart. For in the presence of my father I spoke peaceably to Joseph, but when I had gone out, the spirit of hatred darkened my mind, and stirred up my heart to kill him.

Therefore, you must one another from the heart. If a man sin against you, cast forth the poison of hate and speak peaceably to him, and in thy heart do not hold guile, and if he confess and repent, forgive him.

But if he denies it, do not get into a fight with him, lest, catching the poison from you, he take to cursing and so you sin doubly. And though he deny it, and yet have a sense of shame when reproved, stop reproving him. For he who denies may repent so as not again to wrong you. Yes, he may also honour you and be at peace with you And if he is without shame and persists in his wrong-doing, even so forgive him from the heart, and leave to EL the avenging.

If a man prosperes more than you, do not be troubled by it, but pray also for him, that he may have perfect prosperity. For so it is expedient for you. And if he be further exalted, do not be envious of him, remembering that all flesh shall die; and offer praise to EL, who gives things good and profitable to all men.

Seek out the judgments of Yahua, and your mind will rest and be at peace. And though a man become rich by evil means, even as Esau, the brother of my father, do not be jealous, but wait for the end of Yahua. For if he takes away wealth gotten by evil means, and He forgives him if he repents, but the unrepentant is reserved for eternal punishment. For the poor man who is free from envy pleases Yahua in all things, and is blessed beyond all men, because he does not have the travail of vain men. Put away, therefore, jealousy from your souls, and love one another with uprightness of heart. Therefore, you also must tell these things to your children, that they honor Judah and Levi, for from them shall Yahua raise up salvation to Israel.

And when he had rested for a little while, he said again, "My children, obey your father, and bury me near to my fathers." And he drew up his feet, and fell asleep in peace. And after five years they carried him up to Hebron, and laid him with his fathers.

FATHERS: THE TESTAMENTS OF THE TWELVE PATRIARCHS

# The Testament of Asher

## The Tenth Son of Jacob and Zilpah

T he copy of the Testament of Asher, what things he spake to his sons in the hundred and twenty-fifth year of his life. For while he was still in health, he said to them:

Pay attention, you children of Asher, to your father, and I will declare to you all that is upright in the sight of Yahua.

Two ways has EL given to the sons of men, and two inclinations, and two kinds of action, and two modes (of action), and two issues.

Therefore all things are by twos, one over against the other. For there are two ways of good and evil, and with these are the two inclinations in our breasts discriminating them. Therefore if the soul take pleasure in the good (inclination), all its actions are in righteousness; and if it sin it straightway repents. For, having its thoughts set upon righteousness, and casting away wickedness, it straightway overthrows the evil, and uproots the sin.

But if it incline to the evil inclination, all its actions are in wickedness, and it drives away the good, and cleaves to the evil, and is ruled by Beliar; even though it work what is good, he pervertes it to evil. For whenever it begins to do good, he forces the issue of the action into evil for him, seeing that the treasure of the inclination is filled with an evil spirit.

A person then may with words help the good for the sake of the evil, yet the issue of the action leads to mischief. There is a man who shows no compassion upon him who serves his turn in evil; and this thing has two aspects, but the whole is evil.

And there is a man that loves him that works evil, because he would prefer even to die in evil for his sake; and concerning this it is clear that it has two aspects, but the whole is an evil work. Though indeed he have love, yet is he wicked who conceales what is evil for the sake of the good name, but the end of the action tends to evil.

Another steals, does unjustly, plunders, defrauds, and then after all pities the poor: this too has a twofold aspect, but the whole is evil. He who defrauds his neighbor provokes EL, and swears falsely against the Most High, and yet pities the poor. Yahua, who commands the law, he sets as nothing and provokes Him, and yet he refreshes the poor. He defiles the heart, and makes gay the body. he kills many, and pities a few. This, too, has a twofold aspect, but the whole is evil.

Another committes adultery and fornication, and abstaines from meats, and when he fasts he does evil, and by the power of his wealth overwhelmes many; and notwithstanding his excessive wickedness he does the commandments: this, too, has a twofold aspect, but the whole is evil.

Such men are hares; clean, like those that divide the hoof, but in very deed are unclean. For EL in the tables of the commandments has thus declared.

But do not you, my children, wear two faces like they do, of goodness and of wickedness; but cleave to goodness only, for EL has his habitation therein, and men desire it. But from wickedness flee away, destroying the (evil) inclination by your good works. For they that are double-faced serve not EL, but their own lusts, so that they may please Beliar and men like they are.

For good men, even they that are of single face, though

they be thought by them that are double faced to sin, are just before EL. For many in killing the wicked do two works, of good and evil, but the whole is good because he has uprooted and destroyed that which is evil.

One man hates the merciful and unjust man, and the man who committes adultery and fasts: this, too, has a two fold aspect, but the whole work is good, because he follows Yahua's example, in that he does not accept the seeming good as the genuine good.

Another desires not to see a good day with them that riot, lest he defile his body and pollute his heart. This, too, is double-faced, but the whole is good. For such men are like to stags and to hinds, because in the manner of wild animals they seem to be unclean, but they are altogether clean because they walk in zeal for Yahua and abstain from what EL also hates and forbiddes by His commandments, warding off the evil from the good.

You see, my children, how that there are two in all things, one against the other, and the one is hidden by the other: in wealth (is hidden) covetousness, in conviviality drunkenness, in laughter grief, in wedlock profligacy. Death succeeds to life, dishonour to glory, night to day, and darkness to light; wherefore also eternal life awaits death. Nor may it be said that truth is a lie, nor right wrong; for all truth is under the light, even as all things are under EL. All these things, therefore, I proved in my life, and I wandered not from the truth of Yahua, and I searched out the commandments of the Most High, walking according to all my strength with singleness of face to that which is good.

Therefore, take heed, my children, to the commandments of Yahua, following the truth with singleness of face. For they that are double-faced are guilty of a twofold sin; for they both do the evil thing and they have pleasure in them that do it, following the example of the spirits of deceit, and striving against mankind.

Therefore, my children, keep the law of Yahua, and give no heed to evil as to good; but look to the thing that is really good, and keep it in all commandments of Yahua, having your conversation therein, and resting therein. For the latter ends of men show their righteousness, when they meet the Messengers of the Yahua and of Satan. For when the soul departs troubled, it is tormented by the evil spirit, which also it served in lusts and evil works. But if he is peaceful with joy he meetes the Messenger of peace, and he leads him into eternal life.

Do not become, my children, as Sodom, which sinned against the Messengers of Yahua, and perished for ever. For I know that you shall sin, and be delivered into the hands of your enemies; and your land shall be made desolate, and your holy places destroyed, and you shall be scattered to the four corners of the earth. And you shall be set at nought in the dispersion vanishing away as water until the Most High shall visit the earth, coming Himself.

Therefore, my children, tell these things to your children that they do not disobey Him. For I have known that you shall assuredly be disobedient, and assuredly act wickedly, not giving heed to the law of EL, but to the commandments of men, being corrupted through wickedness. And therefore shall you be scattered as Gad and Dan my brethren, and you shall know not your lands, tribe, and tongue. But Yahua will gather you together in faith through His tender mercy, and for the sake of Abraham, Isaac, and Jacob.

And when he had said these things to them he commanded them, saying, Bury me in Hebron. And he fell asleep and died at a good old age. And his sons did as he had commanded them, and they carried him up to Hebron, and buried him with his fathers.

# The Testament of Joseph

## The Eleventh Son of Jacob and Rachel

The copy of the Testament of Joseph. When he was about to die he called his sons and his brothers together, and said to them:

My brothers and my children, pay attention to Joseph the beloved of Israel. Listen to me, my sons, to your father. I have seen in my life envy and death, Yet I did not go astray, but persevered in the truth of Yahua. These, my brothers, hated me, but Yahua loved me. They wished to kill me, but the EL of my fathers guarded me. They put me down into a pit, and the Most High brought me up again. I was sold into slavery, and Yahua of all made me free. I was taken into captivity, and His strong hand comforted me. I was beset with hunger, and Yahua Himself nourished me. I was alone, and EL comforted me. I was sick, and Yahua visited me. I was in prison, and my EL showed favour to me; in bonds, and He released me; Slandered, and He pleaded my cause. Bitterly spoken against by the Egyptians, and He delivered me. Envied by my fellow-slaves, and He exalted me.

And this chief captain of Pharaoh entrusted to me his house. And I struggled against a shameless woman who urged me repeatedly to transgress with her. But the EL of Israel my father delivered me from the burning flame. I was cast into prison. I was beaten. I was mocked. But Yahua granted for me to find mercy in the sight of the keeper of the prison. For Yahua does not forsake those that fear Him -- neither in darkness, nor in bonds, nor in tribulations, nor in necessities. For EL is not put to shame as a man. nor as the son of man is he afraid, nor as one that is earth-born is He frightened.

But in all those things He gives protection, And in different ways He comforts. Though for a little space He departs to try the inclination of the soul. In ten temptations He showed me approved. And in all of them I endured. For endurance is a mighty charm, and patience gives many good things.

How often did the Egyptian woman threaten me with death? How often did she give me over to punishment, and then call me back and threaten me? And when I was unwilling to company with her, she said to me. "You shall be lord of me, and all that is in my house. if you will give yourself to me, then you shall be as our master."

But I remembered the words of my father, and going into my chamber, I wept and prayed to Yahua. And I fasted in those seven years, and I appeared to the Egyptians as one living delicately, for they that fast for EL's sake receive beauty of face.

And if my lord was away from home, I drank no wine nor for three days did I take my food, but I gave it to the poor and sick. And I sought Yahua early, and I wept for the Egyptian woman of Memphis for very unceasingly did she trouble me. For also at night she came to me under pretence of visiting me, and because she had no male child she pretended to regard me as a son, and so I prayed to Yahua, and she bare a male child. And for a time she embraced me as a son, and I did not know it. But later, she sought to draw me into fornication. And when I perceived it I sorrowed to death. And when she had gone away, I came to myself and lamented for her many days, because I recognized her guile and her deceit. And I declared to her the words of the Most High, if hopefully she would turn from her evil lust.

Often, therefore, she flattered me with words as a holy man, and guilefully in her talk praised my chastity before her husband, while at the same time she desired to trap me when we were alone. For she praised me openly as chaste, but in secret she said to me, "Don't be afraid of my husband because he is persuaded concerning your chastity. And even if someone should tell him concerning us, he would not believe it."

Owing to all these things I lay upon the ground, and besought EL that Yahua would deliver me from her deceit. And when she had prevailed nothing by it, she came again to me under the plea of instruction that she might learn the word of EL.

And she said to me, "If you desire that I should leave my idols, lie with me, and I will persuade my husband to depart from his idols, and we will walk in the law of your Yahua."

And I said to her, "Yahua does not desire that those who reverence Him should be in uncleanness, nor does He take pleasure in them that commit adultery, but in those that approach Him with a pure heart and undefiled lips."

But she held her peace, longing to accomplish her evil desire. And I gave myself even more to fasting and prayer that Yahua might deliver me from her.

And again, at another time she said to me, "If you do not desire to commit adultery, I will kill my husband by poison, and take you to be my husband."

Therefore, when I heard this, I tore my garments, and said to her, "Woman, reverence EL, and do not do this evil deed, unless you be destroyed. For know indeed that I will declare this your device to all men."

She therefore, being fraid, begged me that I would not declare this device. And she departed soothing me with gifts, and sending to me every delight of the sons of men.

And afterward she sent me food mingled with enchantments. But when the eunuch who brought it came, I looked up and saw a terrible man giving me with the dish a sword, and I perceived that (her) scheme was to beguile me. And when he had gone out I wept, nor did I taste that or any other of her food.

So after one day she came to me and observed the food, and said to me, "Why is it that you have not eaten of the food?"

And I said to her, "It is because you have filled it with deadly enchantments; and how can you say 'I come not near to idols, but to Yahua alone?' Therefore know now that the EL of my father revealed to me by His Messenger your wickedness, and I have kept it to convict you, if hopefully you may see and repent. So that you may learn that the wickedness of the ungodly has no power over them that worship EL with chastity, Look now -- I will take it and eat it before your eyes."

And having said this, I then prayed, "The EL of my fathers and the Messenger of Abraham, be with me."

And ate.

And when she saw this she fell upon her face at my feet, weeping. And I raised her up and admonished her. And she promised to do this iniquity no more.

But her heart was still set upon evil, and she looked around how to trap me, and sighing deeply she became downcast, though she was not sick.

And when her husband saw her, he said to her, "Why are you so sad?"

And she said to him, "I have a pain at my heart, and the groanings of my spirit oppress me."

And so he comforted her who was not sick.

Then, accordingly seizing an opportunity, she rushed to me while her husband was yet outside, and said to me,

"I will hang myself, or cast myself over a cliff, if you will not lie with me."

And when I saw the spirit of Beliar was troubling her, I prayed to Yahua, and said to her, "Why, wretched woman, are you troubled and disturbed, blinded through sins? Remember that if you kill yourself, Asteho, the concubine of your husband, your rival, will beat your children, and you will destroy your memorial from off the earth."

And she said to me, "Aha, then you love me! Let this suffice me. Only fight for my life and my children, and I expect that I shall enjoy my desire also."

But she did not know that because of my Yahua I spoke these things, and not because of her. For if a man falls before the passion of a wicked desire and becomes enslaved by it, even as she, whatever good thing he may hear with regard to that passion, he receives it with a view to his wicked desire.

Therefore, I declare to you, my children, that it was about the sixth hour when she walk away from me; and I knelt before Yahua all day, and all the night; and about dawn I rose up, weeping the entire time and praying for a release from her.

At last, then, she laid hold of my garments, forcibly dragging me to have sex with her. And when I saw that in her madness she held tight to my garment, I left it behind, and fled away naked. And while holding the garment she falsely accused me, and when her husband came he cast me into prison in his house. And on the next day he beat me and sent me into Pharaoh's prison.

And when I was in bonds, the Egyptian woman was oppressed with grief, and she came and heard how I gave thanks to Yahua and sang praises in the dark prison. And with glad voice I rejoiced, glorifying my EL that I was delivered from the lustful desire of the Egyptian woman.

And often she sent to me saying, "Agree to fulfill my desire, and I will release you from your bonds, and free you from the darkness."

And not even in thought did I incline to her. For EL loves him who in a den of wickedness combines fasting with chastity, rather than the man who in kings' chambers combines luxury with licence. And if a man lives in chastity, and desires also glory, and the Most High knows that it is expedient for him, He bestows this also upon me.

How often, though she were sick, did she come down to me at unlooked for times, and listened to my voice as I prayed! And when I heard her groanings I held my peace. For when I was in her house she would bare her arms, and breasts, and legs, that I might lie with her. For she was very beautiful and splendidly adorned in order to beguile me. But Yahua guarded me from her devices.

You see, therefore, my children, how great things patience works, and prayer with fasting. So to you too, if you follow after chastity and purity with patience and prayer, with fasting in humility of heart, will Yahua dwell among you because He loves chastity. And wherever the Most High dwells, even though envy, or slavery, or slander befall (a man), Yahua who dwells in him, for the sake of his chastity, not only delivers him from evil, but also exalts him even as He did me.

For in every way the man is lifted up, whether in deed, or in word, or in thought. My brothers knew how my father loved me, and yet I did not exalt myself in my mind. Although I was a child, I had the fear of EL in my heart. For I knew that all things would pass away. And I did not raise myself (against them) with evil intent, but I honored my brothers. And out of respect for them, even when I was being sold, I refrained from telling the Ishmaelites that I was a son of Jacob, a great man and a mighty.

Do you also, my children, have the fear of EL in all

your works before your eyes, and honor your brothers. For every one who does the law of Yahua shall be loved by Him.

And when I came to the Indocolpitae with the Ishmaelites, they asked me, saying: "Are you a slave?"

And I said that I was a home-born slave, that I might not put my brothers to shame.

And the eldest of them and said to me, "You are not a slave, for even your appearance tells me that."

But I said that I was their slave.

Now when we came into Egypt they fought about me concerning which of 5 them should buy me and take me. Therefore it seemed good to all that I should remain in Egypt with the merchant of their trade, until they should return bringing merchandise. And Yahua gave me favor in the eyes of the merchant, and he entrusted to me his house. And EL blessed  him by my means, and increased him in gold and silver and in household servants. And I was with him three months and five days.

And about that time the Memphian woman, the wife of Pentephri, came down in a chariot, with great pomp, because she had heard from her eunuchs concerning me. And she told her husband that the merchant had become rich by means of a young Hebrew, and they said, "He has certainly been stolen out of the land of Canaan. Now, therefore, render justice to him, and take away the youth to your house; so shall the EL of the Hebrews bless your, for grace from heaven is upon him."

And Pentephris was persuaded by her words, and commanded the merchant to be brought, and said to him, "What is this that I hear about you that you steal persons out of the land of Canaan, and sell them for slaves?"

But the merchant fell at his feet, and pleaded with him, saying, "I beg you, my lord. I know nothing about what you are saying."

And Pentephris said to him, "Where, then, did this Hebrew slave come from?"

And he said, "The Ishmaelites entrusted him to me until they should return."

But he did not believe him, amd commanded him to be stripped and beaten. And when he persisted in this statement, Pentephris said, "Bring the youth to me."

And when I was brought in, I humbled myself before Pentephris (for he was third in rank of the officers of Pharaoh). And he took me apart from him, and said to me. "Are you a slave or free?"

And I said, "A slave."

And he said, "Whose?"

And I said, "The Ishmaelites."

And he asked, "How did you become their slave?"

And I answered, "They bought me out of the land of Canaan."

And he said to me, "Truly you lie!" and strightway he commanded me to be stripped and beaten.

Now the Memphian woman was looking through a window at me while I was being beaten, for her house was near, and she sent to him saying, "Your judgement is unjust; for you  punish a free man who has been stolen as though he were a transgressor."

And when I made no change in my statement, though I was beaten, he ordered me to be imprisoned, until, as he said, "the owners  of the boy should come."

And the woman said to her husband, "For what reason do you detain the captive and well-born lad in bonds who ought rather to be set free, and be waited upon?"

For she wished to see me out of a desire of sin, but I was ignorant concerning all these things.

And he said to her, "It is not the custom of the Egyptians to take that which belong to others before proof is given." This, therefore, he said concerning the merchant;

"and as for the lad, he must be imprisoned."

Now after twenty-four days the Ishmaelites came because they had heard that Jacob my father was mourning much concerning me. And they came and said to me, "How is it that you said that you were a slave? Now look, we have learned that you are the son of a mighty man in the land of Canaan, and your father still mourns for you in sackcloth and ashes."

When I heard this my bowels were dissolved and my heart melted, and I desired greatly to weep, but I restrained myself, that I should not put my brothers to shame. And I said to them, "I don't know. I am a slave."

Therefore, they then took counsel to sell me that I should not be found in their hands. For they feared my father, lest he [should come and] execute upon them a grievous vengeance. For they had heard that he was mighty with EL and with men.

Then said the merchant to them, "Release me from the judgment of Pentiphri."

And they came and requested of me, saying, "Say that you were bought by us with money, and he will set us free."

Now the Memphian woman said to her husband, "Buy the youth; for I hear that they are selling him."

And straightway she sent a eunuch to the Ishmaelites, and asked them to sell me. But since the eunuch would not agree to buy me (at their price) he returned, having made an offer to buy from them. So he made known to his mistress that they asked a large price for their slave.

And she sent another eunuch, saying, "Even if they demand two minas, give it to them. Do not spare the gold. Only buy the boy, and bring him to me."

So the eunuch went and gave them eighty pieces of gold, and he bought me. But to the Egyptian woman he said, "I have given a hundred."

And though I knew the truth, I held my peace, unless the eunuch should be put to shame.

You see, therefore, my children, what great things I endured that I should not put my brothers to shame. Do you also, therefore love one another, and with long-suffering hide one another's faults. For EL delights in the unity of brothers, and in the purpose of a heart that takes pleasure in love.

And when my brothers came into Egypt they learnrf that I had returned their money to them, and did not blame them, and comforted them. And after the death of Jacob my father I loved them more abundantly, and all things whatsoever he commanded I did very abundantly for them, And I did not allow them to be afflicted in the smallest matter. And all that was in my hand I gave to them. And their children were my children, and my children as their servants. And their life was my life, and all their suffering was my suffering, and all their sickness was my sickness. My land was their land, and their counsel my counsel. And I did not exalt myself among them in arrogance because of my worldly glory, but I was among them as one of the least.

If you also, therefore, walk in the commandments of Yahua, my children, He will exalt you there, and will bless you with good things for ever and ever. And if any one seeks to do evil to you, do well to him, and pray for him, and you shall be redeemed of Yahua from all evil. [For], behold, you see that out of my humility and long-suffering I took to wife the daughter of the priest of Heliopolis. And a hundred talents of gold were given me with her, and Yahua made them to serve me. And He gave me also beauty as a flower beyond the beautiful ones of Israel; and He preserved me to old age in strength and in beauty, because I was like in all things to Jacob.

Hear me, therefore, about my vision which I saw.

I saw twelve harts feeding. And nine of them were dispersed. Now the three were preserved, but on the following day they also were dispersed.

And I saw that the three harts became three lambs, and they cried to Yahua, and He brought them forth into a flourishing and well watered place. He brought them out of darkness into light. And there they cried to Yahua until there gathered together to them the nine harts, and they became as twelve sheep, and after a little time they increased and became many flocks.

And after these things I saw and behold, twelve bulls were sucking one cow, which produced a sea of milk, and there drank thereof the twelve flocks and innumerable herds. And the horns of the fourth bull went up to heaven and became as a wall for the flocks, and in the midst of the two horns there grew another horn. And I saw a bull calf which surrounded them twelve times, and it became a help to the bulls wholly.

And I saw in the midst of the horns a virgin [wearing a many-coloured garment, and from her] went forth a lamb; and on his right (was as it were a lion; and) all the beasts and all the reptiles rushed (against him), and the lamb over came them and destroyed them. And the bulls rejoiced because of him, and the cow [and the harts] exulted together with them. And these things must come to pass in their season.

Do you therefore, my children, observe the commandments of Yahua, and honour Levi and Judah; for from them shall arise to you one who saves Israel. For His kingdom is an everlasting kingdom, which shall not pass away; but my kingdom among you shall come to an end as a watcher's hammock, which after the summer disappeareth.

THE TESTAMENT OF JOSEPH

For I know that after my death the Egyptians will afflict you, but EL will avenge you, and will bring you into that which He promised to your fathers. But you shall carry up my bones with you; for when my bones are being taken up thither, Yahua shall be with you in light, and Beliar shall be in darkness with the Egyptians.

And carry you up Asenath your mother to the Hippodrome, and near Rachel your mother bury her.

And when he had said these things he stretched out his feet, and died at a good old age. And all Israel mourned for him, and all Egypt, with a great mourning. And when the children of Israel went out of Egypt, they took with them the bones of Joseph, and they buried him in Hebron with his fathers, and the years of his life were one hundred and ten years.

# The Testament of Benjamin

## The Twelfth Son of Jacob and Rachel

T he copy of the words of Benjamin, which he commanded his sons to observe, after he had lived a hundred and twenty-five years. And he kissed them, and said:

As Isaac was born to Abraham in his old age, so also was I to Jacob. And since Rachel my mother died in giving me birth, I had no milk; therefore I was nursed by Bilhah her handmaid. For Rachel remained barren for twelve years after she had borne Joseph; and she prayed Yahua with fasting twelve days, and she conceived and bare me. For my father loved Rachel dearly and prayed that he might see two sons born from her. Therefore I was called Benjamin, that is, "a son of days."

And when I went into Egypt to Joseph, my brother recognized me, he said to me: "What did they tell my father when they sold me?"

And I said to him, "They dabbled your coat with blood and sent it, and said: 'Do you know whether this be your son's coat?'"

And Joseph said to me, "Even so, brother, the 'Canaanite merchants' [his brothers] stole me by force, and it came to pass that as they went on their way they hid my garment, and claimed a wild beast had met me and slain me."

And so 'his associates' sold him to the Ishmaelites. And he did not lie in saying this. For he wished to hide from me the deeds of my brothers. And he called to him his brothers and said, "Do not tell my father what you have done to me, but tell him as I have told Benjamin. And let the thoughts among you be such, and let not these things come to the heart of my father."

Therefore, also, my children, love Yahua, the EL of heaven and earth, and keep His commandments, following the example of the good and holy man Joseph. And let your mind be to good, even as you know me, for he that has his mind right sees all things rightly.

Fear Yahua, and love your neighbor, and even though the spirits of Beliar claim you to afflict you with every evil, yet they shall not have dominion over you, even as they did not have over Joseph my brother.

How many men wished to kill him, but EL shielded him! For he that fears EL and loves his neighbor cannot be smitten by the spirit of Beliar, because he is shielded by the fear of EL.

Nor can he be ruled over by the device of men or beasts, for he is helped by Yahua through the love that he has towards his neighbor. For Joseph also besought our father that he would pray for his brothers, that Yahua would not impute to them as sin because of the evil they had done to him.

And thus Jacob cried out, "My good child, you prevailed over the bowels of you father Jacob." And he embraced him, and kissed him for two hours, saying, "In you shall be fulfilled the prophecy of heaven that a blameless one shall be delivered up for lawless men, and a sinless one shall die for wicked men.

Do you see, my children, the end of the good man? Therefore, be followers of his compassion with a good mind that you also may wear crowns of glory. For the good man does not have a dark eye for he shows mercy to all men, even though they are sinners. And though they with intent devise evil concerning him, by doing good he overcomes evil being shielded by EL.

He loves the righteous as his own soul. If any one is glorified, he does not envy him. If any one is enriched, he is not jealous. If any one is valiant, he praises him. He praises the virtuous man, and on the poor man he has mercy. On the weak he has compassion. To EL he sings praises.

As for him who has the fear of EL, he protects him as with a shield. Whoever loves EL he helps. He that rejects the Most High he admonishes and turns back. And he who has the grace of a good spirit, he loves as his own soul.

Therefore, if you also have a good mind, then both wicked men will be at peace with you and the profligate will reverence you and turn to good. The covetous will not only cease from their inordinate desire, but even give the objects of their covetousness to them that are afflicted.

If you do well, even the unclean spirits will flee from you, and the beasts will fear you. For where there is reverence for good works and light in the mind, even darkness flees away from him. For if any one does violence to a holy man, he repents for the holy man is merciful to his reviler, and holds his peace. And if any one betrays a righteous man, the righteous man prays: though for a little time he is humbled, yet not long after he appears far more glorious, as was Joseph my brother.

The inclinations of the good man is not in the power of the deceit of the spirit of Beliar, for the Messenger of peace guides his heart, and he does not gaze passionately upon corruptible things, nor gather together riches through a desire of pleasure. He does not delight in pleasure. He does not satiate himself with luxuries. He errs not in the uplifting of the eyes. Yahua is his portion.

The good inclined does not receive glory nor dishonor from men, and does not know guile or lies or fighting or reviling. Yahua dwells in him and lights up his heart, and he rejoices towards all men always.

He with good mind does not have two tongues, of blessing and of cursing, of contempt and of honor, of sorrow and of joy, of quietness and of confusion, of hypocrisy and of truth, but he has one disposition, uncorrupt and pure concerning all men. He has no double sight nor double hearing for in everything which he does, or speaks, or sees, he knows that Yahua looks on the heart. And he cleanses his mind that he may not be condemned by men as well as by EL.

And in like manner the works of Beliar are twofold, and there is no singleness in them. Therefore, my children, I tell you, flee the malice of Beliar for he gives a sword to them that obey him, and the sword is the mother of seven evils because the mind conceives through Beliar, and then first (of the seven evils) is bloodshed; second: ruin; third: tribulation; fourth: exile; fifth: lack; sixth: panic; and seventh: destruction.

Therefore Cain was also delivered over to seven vengeances by EL for in every hundred years Yahua brought one plague upon him. And when he was two hundred years old he began to suffer this way, and in the nine-hundredth year he was destroyed. On the account of Abel, his brother, Cain was judged with all the evils. But Lamech with seventy times seven because for ever those who are like Cain in envy and hatred of brothers shall be punished with the same judgment.

And you, my children, flee evil-doing, envy, and hatred of brothers, and cleave to goodness and love. He that has a pure mind in love does not look at a woman with a view to fornication for he has no defilement in his heart because the Spirit of EL rests upon him. For as the sun is not defiled by shining on dung and mire, but rather dries up both and drives away the evil smell, so also the pure mind, though encompassed by the defilements of earth, is cleansed and is not itself defiled.

And I believe that there will be also evil-doings among you, from the words of Enoch the righteous that you shall commit fornication with the fornication of Sodom, and shall perish, except for a few, and shall renew evil deeds with women, and the kingdom of Yahua shall not be among you, for straightway He shall take it away.

Nevertheless the temple of EL shall be in your portion, and the last (temple) shall be more glorious than the first. And the twelve tribes shall be gathered together there, and all the Gentiles, until the Most High shall send forth His salvation in the visitation of an only begotten prophet.

Now when Joseph was in Egypt, I longed to see his figure and the form of his countenance; and through the prayers of Jacob my father I saw him, while awake in the daytime, even his entire figure exactly as he was.

And when he had said these things, he said to them:

Know you, therefore, my children, that I am dying. Therefore , do truth and righteousness each one to his neighbor, and judgment to confirmation, and keep the law of Yahua and his commandments. For these things I leave you instead of inheritance.

Therefore,  give them to your children for an everlasting possession for so did Abraham, and Isaac, and Jacob. All these things they gave us for an inheritance, saying, "Keep the commandments of EL until Yahua shall reveal His salvation to all Gentiles. And then shall you see Enoch, Noah, and Shem, and Abraham, Isaac, and Jacob, rising on the right hand in gladness. Then shall we also rise, each one over our tribe, worshipping the King of heaven,

Then also all men shall rise, some to glory and some to shame. And Yahua shall judge Israel first for their unrighteousness. And He shall convict Israel through the chosen ones of the nations even as He reproved Esau through the Midianites who deceived their brothers, becoming therefore children in the portion of them that fear Yahua.

Therefore, if you, my children, walk in holiness according to the commandments of Yahua, you shall again dwell securely with me, and all Israel shall be gathered to Yahua. And I shall no longer be called a ravening wolf because of your ravages.

And when he finished his words, he said, "I command you, my children, carry up my bones out of Egypt, and bury me at Hebron, near my fathers."

So Benjamin died a hundred and twenty-five years old at a good old age, and they placed him in a coffin. And in the ninety-first year from the entrance of the children of Israel into Egypt, they and their brothers brought up the bones of their fathers secretly during the Canaanite war. They buried them in Hebron by the feet of their fathers. And they returned from the land of Canaan and dwelt in Egypt until the day of their departure from the land of Egypt.

# Epilogue

T housands of years later we still have the words of the Fathers. Not only these fathers, but also our father Enoch. The Plant of Righteousness has come to a decision point, a crossroads. Enoch was given a vision and dream of seven "*weeks*" that, according to the context of the vision, each week shows us that these are really *ages*. Each age has been marked by events that happened during or at the close of the age.

The age in which we live is the seventh.

> And after that (the sixth age) in the seventh week an apostate generation will arise. Its deeds will be many, and all its deeds will be apostate.
>
> And at its close will be set apart the elect righteous of the eternal Plant of Righteousness to receive sevenfold instruction concerning all His creation. Enoch 93:9-10

The patriarchs who gave their testaments included prophecies of what might happen to their "children" at the "end of the days." Problems would happen during this time unless they chose to follow the Instructions of Yahua (the Torah) and learn to trust EL (The one from whom all things ultimately came).

Enoch in the above prophecy about the time in which we live was told that something was going to happen to the "elect righteous" who are from the offspring of those who gave the testaments.

First, they would be "set apart."

Second, they are the "elect righteous" or "chosen" out of the Plant of Righteousness.

Third, they would be given "instruction concerning" all of His (Yahua's) creation.

What does this mean?

First, how are these "set apart?" The apparent answer is amazing and shocking.

How would the "elect righteous of the Plant of Righteousness" be set apart from the rest of the world? After thousands of years and dispersions of the Plant of Righteous among all the nations of the world, how would they be recognized as being different from anyone else? Would their appearance change, like growing a third eye?

No, something else is going to happen, not just to these, but to every person in the world.

Here is another prophecy that was given through Joel ("Yahua is EL"):

**First there is the warning that the Day of Yahua is near and what to expect**

Blow the rams horn in Zion, and sound the alarm in my set apart mountain! Let all the inhabitants of the earth tremble, for the day of Yahua is coming, for it is near.

A day of darkness and gloom, a day of clouds and thick darkness, like the morning clouds spread over the mountains – a people many and strong, the like of whom has never been, nor shall there ever be again after them, to the years of many generations.

Ahead of them a fire has consumed and behind them a flame burns. Before them the land is like the Garden of Eden, and behind them a desert waste. And from them there is no escape.

Their appearance is like the appearance of horses, and they run like steeds. As the noise of chariots, they leap over the mountaintops, as the noise of a flaming fire consuming stubble, as a mighty people set in battle array. Before them people are in anguish, all faces become flushed. They run like mighty men. They climb the wall like men of battle, everyone goes on his way, and they do not break ranks. And they do not press on another, and everyone goes on his own path. They fall among the weapons, but they do not stop. They rush on the city. They run on the wall. They climb into houses. They enter at the windows like a thief.

The earth shall tremble before them. The heavens shall shake. Sun and moon shall be darkened, and the stars shall withdraw their brightness.

And Yahua shall raise His voice before His army, for his camp is very great, for mighty is the doer of His word.

For the day of Yahua is great and very awesome, and who can bear it? (From Joel 2 -- The Scriptures)

The following was also written by our father Enoch, and quoted by Jude in the New Testament:

The Messengers showed me. From them I heard everything, and from them I understood as I saw, but NOT for this generations (Enoch's), but for a remote one, which is to come. Concerning the elect I took up (understood) my parables (I heard) concerning them, and [the Messenger] said:

The set apart Great One will come from His dwelling. The eternal One of EL will tread upon the earth, and appear from his camp in the strength of His might from the Heaven of heavens.

And all will be struck with fear, and the Watchers will tremble. Great fear and trembling will seize them.

To the ends of the earth, the high mountains will be shaken, and the high hills will be made low, and melt like wax before the flame. The earth will be wholly torn up, and all living things on the earth will die. A judgment will be upon all.

But with the righteous He will make peace and will protect the chosen (elect), and mercy will be on them. And they will all belong to EL, and they will be prospered, and they will all be blessed. He will help them all. And light will appear to them, and He will make peace with them.

And look! He comes with ten thousands of His set apart ones to exercise judgment on all, and to destroy all the ungodly, and to convict all flesh of the works of their ungodliness that they have ungodly committed, and of all the hard things that the ungodly sinners have spoken against Him. (From Enoch 1. - Enoch: The Book Behind the Bible}

We are surrounded by a "great crowd of witnesses" concerning the Day of Yahua. Therefore, it would do us well to pay close attention to this next section, because this is what happens BEFORE all of this comes on the earth and its people.

Before the Day of Yahua the people of the earth will be made ready for it. But probably not in the way one might think.

At the time of this writing troubles are beginning to afflict all nations. None are left out. The United States, supposed to be the bastion of peace and strength now suffers under a cloud of confusion and corruption. The leaders and the people don't know where to turn. What they attempt to do only results in hatching viper's eggs, and it doesn't matter which political party is involved. From the head to the feet, there is only infectious boils. The people fear "Their hope is cut off." Who is not contaminated by the flood of lies that threaten to sink all regardless of party, race, religion, age, or sex? The world is sinking in the mire and quicksand, and no one can rescue.

We need a deliverer, but instead we put our trust in horribly flawed princes, who make promises with poisonous words, which the people drink in like a side-show barker's miracle elixir.

We search for answers, but find none. We cry for help, but no one listens. We plead for change, but the change is worse than before.

Enoch began his book with the quote above. He ended his book with a long section that distinguished the difference between the right-doers and wrong-doers. It was not simply trying to make a distinction between them, but rather to show how each will fare in the end.

Many who think they are "righteous" are not. And many who think they are "wrong-doers" are not. The world thinks that black is white, and white is black, that darkness is light, and light is darkness, that the truth is a lie and that lies (and opinions) are truth.

Therefore, does it not seem reasonable that something should happen to turn this upside down world, upright?

First, let me explain. I used the Name "Yahua" which is really made of four ancient Hebrew vowels, and when sung would sound like this: "*ee - - ah -- oo -- ahhh.*" And every singer knows that the tone is carried by the vowels, but in solid tone, produced by singing vowels, certain consonants are automatically produced as one moves from vowel to vowel: "*ee -- (y) -- ah -- (h) -- oo -- (w) -- ahhhh.*" So that Name ("that must not be said") is *Yahua.* However, the time of "not saying or singing the Name" is OVER!

But before we can say the Name, we must know what we are saying. It is an important physical and spiritual sound, but its meaning is what counts. It means "He Exists!" The fathers of the book learned in some cases early on and others after some trials that He Exists! When they came to grips with this awakening, their lives changed. And this change they passed on to their children and down to us living at this time.

The world will find out soon that He Exists! But they will have a chance to understand this before the armies of heaven are sent.

## Yahua will restore His Identity to His People

If you don't know something, then you don't even know that you don't know. When the subject comes up for which there has never been any interest, then the mind goes blank and continues on to other thoughts. But what would happen if suddenly you began thinking about subjects, words, names, images, events and any other thoughts that are related to an unknown topic?

The Day of Yahua will come, because He Exists! But before that happens He will make Himself known to His People. They will receive insight and understanding, and they WILL understand. But the wrong doers will continue to do wrong, and none of them will understand -- even if they, with Israel, receive the Spirit of Yahua. Joel 2 continues ...

> Blow a ram's horn in Zion. Set apart a fast. Call an assembly. Gather the people. Set the assembly apart. Assemble the elders. Gather the children and nursing babes. Let a bridegroom come out from his room, and a bride from her dressing room.
>
> Let the priests, servants of Yahua, weep between the porch and the altar. And let them say, *"Spare Your people,*

*Oh Yahua, and do not give Your inheritance to reproach, for the gentiles to rule over them. Why should they say among the peoples, 'Where is their Elohim?' And let Yahua be jealous for His land, and spare His people. And let Yahua answer and say to His people:* **'See, I am sending you the grain and the new wine and the oil, and you shall be satisfied by them. And no longer do I make you a reproach among the gentiles. And the Northerner I shall remove far from you, and drive him away into a dry and deserted land, with his face toward the eastern sea and his rear toward the western sea. And his stench shall come up and his smell rise, for he has done greatly.'"**

Do not fear, Oh soil, be glad and rejoice, for Yahua has done greatly! Do not fear, you beasts of the field, for the pastures of the wilderness shall spring forth, and the tree shall bear its fruit, the fig tree and the vine shall yield their strength. And you children of Zion, be glad and rejoice in Yahua of Elohim, for He shall give you the Teacher of Righteousness, and cause the rain to come down for you, the former rain and the latter rain, as before. And the threshing-floors shall be filled with grain, and the vats shall overflow with new wine and oil.

**"Then I shall repay you the years that the swarming locust has eaten, the crawling locust, and the consuming locust, and the gnawing locust, My great army which I sent among you."**

Then you shall eat  and be satisfied – and shall praise the Name of Yahua your Elohim, who has done with you so wondrously.

**"And you shall know that I am in the midst of Israel, and that I am Yahua your Elohim and there is no one else. And My people shall never be put to shame.**

**"And after this it shall be that I pour out My Spirit on all flesh. And your sons and your daughters shall prophesy, your old men dream dreams, your young men see visions. And also on the male servants and on the female servants**

**I shall pour out My Spirit in those days.**

"And I shall give signs in the heavens and upon the earth: blood and fire and columns of smoke, the sun is turned into darkness, and the moon into blood, BEFORE the coming of the great and awesome day of Yahua."

*And it shall be that everyone who calls on the Name of Yahua (He Exists!) shall be delivered. For on Mount Zion and in Jerusalem there shall be an escape as Yahua has said, and among the survivors whom Yahua calls.*

Breinigsville, PA USA
21 June 2010
240259BV00001B/2/P